JESUS

JESUS

A

HISTORICAL

PORTRAIT

DANIEL J. HARRINGTON, s.j.

ST. ANTHONY MESSENGER PRESS
Cincinnati, Ohio

Permission to Publish:
Carl K. Moeddel,
Vicar General and Auxiliary Bishop,
Archdiocese of Cincinnati,
October 3, 2005—July 24, 2006

The permission to publish is a declaration that a book or pamphlet is considered to be free from doctrinal or moral error. It is not implied that those who have granted the permission to publish agree with the contents, opinions or statements expressed.

The Scripture quotations contained herein are from the *New Revised Standard Version Bible: Catholic Edition,* copyright ©1989, 1993, Division of Christian Education of the National Council of the Churches of Christ in the United States of America. Used by permission. All rights reserved.

Cover and book design by Mark Sullivan
Cover photo © www.istockphoto.com/Richard Paul Kane

LIBRARY OF CONGRESS CATALOGING-IN-PUBLICATION DATA
Harrington, Daniel J.
Jesus : a historical portrait / Daniel J. Harrington.
p. cm.
Includes bibliographical references and index.
ISBN 978-0-86716-833-4 (pbk. : alk. paper) 1. Jesus Christ—Person and offices. I. Title.

BT203.H37 2007
232.9'01—dc22
[B]
                                        2007011424

ISBN: 978-0-86716-833-4

Published by St. Anthony Messenger Press
28 W. Liberty St.
Cincinnati, OH 45202
www.AmericanCatholic.org

Printed in the United States of America
Printed on acid-free paper
07 08 09 10 11   5 4 3 2 1

CONTENTS

INTRODUCTION

Two thousand years after his death Jesus of Nazareth continues to be the object of fascination, devotion and controversy. While the churches try to carry on the traditions of Christian faith, the popular news media gives ample publicity to new (and often preposterous) explanations about who Jesus really was. What gets ignored in these controversies are the solid scholarly works that place Jesus in his proper historical context and sift the evidence to arrive at a reliable and coherent interpretation of what Jesus said and did.

This book aims to state concisely and clearly for a general audience what many specialists in biblical research have learned and written about Jesus of Nazareth in recent years. It is a historical study, though it has theological significance. Historians try to understand the world of Jesus and to situate him in the context of first-century Judaism. They also act as detectives by going behind the ancient literary sources about Jesus and seeking to ascertain what can be said about him with confidence.

Why not just read the four Gospels? Of course we must read them. The Gospels and other New Testament writings answer two basic questions: *Who is Jesus?* and *Why is he important?* They remain the principal and indispensable sources of our knowledge about Jesus, and without them modern historians could say little or nothing.

However, the Gospels were written after and in the light of Easter, and their authors and first readers already believed in and revered Jesus as the Messiah, Son of God and Lord. They were composed to increase and deepen faith in the risen Jesus, not to give a precise chronicle of Jesus' life on earth. They must be read on three levels: as reports about the time of the earthly Jesus, as reflections of the traditions about Jesus that were handed on in the early churches, and as finished compositions by the Evangelists. This complex process of transmission took about sixty years.

This book is mainly concerned with the time of Jesus, that is, what can be said with a high degree of probability about his life, teachings and activities during his earthly existence. It treats his historical context in Judaism, his birth and the beginnings of his ministry, what he taught and did, his attitudes toward and interactions with women and political leaders, and why and how he died. It also discusses his resurrection, the rise of devotion to him after his death and expectations about his future or second coming.

I intend this short portrait of the historical Jesus as a reliable synthesis of and a positive contribution to recent discussions and controversies about Jesus. I write as a Roman Catholic priest, a Jesuit and a professor of New Testament since 1971. In my academic research I have taken special interest in the Dead Sea Scrolls and other Jewish texts from the time of Jesus. As editor of *New Testament Abstracts* I see all the books and articles published in the field. There is nothing in this book that poses a threat to Christian faith and tradition. Indeed, in most cases it shows that sound historical study is consistent with orthodox Christian beliefs.

The main text of the book appeared first as a series of twelve newsletters published from March 2006 through February 2007 by St. Anthony Messenger Press under the same title as this book. It includes the sidebars ("Adding to the Picture") written by Diane Houdek, as well as questions for reflection and discussion for each chapter. I have added as an appendix an essay entitled "Jesus and the Dead Sea Scrolls" and a list of what I regard as some of the best recent books on the historical Jesus. I am grateful to Judy Ball, Lisa Biedenbach and their colleagues at St. Anthony Messenger Press for their encouragement, editorial skill and efficiency.

CHAPTER ONE

• *How Do We Know Who Jesus Is?* •

T he question of Jesus' identity is central to us as Christians.
Because Christianity is an incarnational faith—centered on Jesus,
the Word of God who became flesh and dwelt among us—it is
important to learn as much as we can about the Jesus of history. He
lived in the land of Israel during what we now call the first century.
The question of his identity still has great relevance for us in the
early twenty-first century. Just consider the recent media attention
received by Mel Gibson's film *The Passion of the Christ* and Dan
Brown's novel *The Da Vinci Code.*

When Jesus asked his disciples, "Who do people say that I am?"
he got several different answers: John the Baptist, Elijah, one of the
prophets. Even when Peter identified Jesus correctly as the Messiah,
Jesus felt the need to redefine messiahship in terms of his coming
passion, death and resurrection.

A Difficult Question

Although important, the question about Jesus' identity is difficult to answer. It is hard to know the whole story about any person, even someone who has lived in our own time, let alone someone who lived two thousand years ago.

The major sources about Jesus—the Gospels of Matthew, Mark, Luke and John—were written in light of the authors' convictions about Jesus' resurrection and continued existence with the one whom he called "Father." The claims that these authors made about Jesus (such as "Jesus is Lord") go beyond what is said about even the greatest human heroes.

My goal in this book is to state what, in my judgment, current New Testament scholarship allows us to say with confidence about Jesus as a historical figure. I want to tell the "honest truth" about what we can know about Jesus of Nazareth and thus provide a reasonably objective account against which the claims of Mel Gibson, Dan Brown and others can be measured.

Major Sources

The four Gospels are the major sources for what we know about Jesus. Nevertheless, they do not allow us to write a full biography about him. Rather, the evangelists were primarily interested in Jesus' religious significance and his impact as a moral figure.

Mark's Gospel, written around AD 70, perhaps in Rome, tells the story of Jesus' public ministry in Galilee, his journey with his disciples to Jerusalem and his short ministry there as well as his passion, death and resurrection. Mark gave special attention to Jesus as the suffering Messiah and to the mystery of the cross.

Around AD 85–90 Matthew and Luke seem to have independently produced their own revised and expanded versions of Mark's Gospel. They added a large amount of teaching material from other sources and traditions. Matthew emphasized the Jewishness of Jesus and his fulfillment of Israel's Scriptures, the books of the Bible Christians commonly call the Old Testament. Luke stressed Jesus' significance not only for Israel but also for the other peoples of the world. Because the first three Gospels offer a common outline and vision of Jesus, they are often called the Synoptic Gospels, meaning "viewed with one eye or lens" or offering a common vision. While John's Gospel has much in common with the Synoptic Gospels and contains many pieces of solid historical information, it spreads the public ministry of Jesus over three years instead of one, introduces different characters and focuses more on Jesus as the revealer and revelation of God than on the kingdom. These four Gospels became part of the church's list of approved books (canon) because of their wide use, orthodox theological content and association with the apostles.

Other Sources
The noncanonical gospels attributed to Thomas, Peter, Mary Magdalene, Philip and others did not become part of the church's New Testament canon. This was due in part to their lack of wide usage, sometimes unorthodox theological content and relatively late dates of composition.

These sources now often serve as the basis for works like *The Da Vinci Code* and other, often sensational, interpretations of early Christianity—some even by well-known scholars. They may contain some early authentic traditions, though it is often difficult to isolate these from their less credible content. Likewise, while there are stray sayings attributed to Jesus in other early Christian writings, it is almost impossible to prove they originated with Jesus.

The only substantial ancient description of Jesus apart from Christian sources appears in the *Jewish Antiquities* by Flavius Josephus, a Jewish historian in the late first century AD. But explicit statements about Jesus' identity as the Messiah and about his resurrection suggest that Christian scribes may have inserted their own convictions about Jesus.

About this time arose Jesus, a wise man, if indeed it be lawful to call him a man. For he was a doer of wonderful deeds, and a teacher of men who...drew to himself many both of the Jews and the Gentiles. He was the Christ....[1]

Gospel Development

The early Christians were more concerned with experiencing the risen Jesus and the Holy Spirit than with writing books about Jesus. Jesus died around AD 30, and the first complete Gospel (Mark's) appeared forty years later. In those intervening decades there was a lively process in which traditions from and about Jesus, whether in oral or written form, were passed on among Christians. These traditions were often shaped and reshaped in response to the pastoral needs of the communities.

Understanding the process by which the Gospels were formed requires keeping three realities in mind: (1) the focus of the evangelist, (2) the development of the early church and (3) who Jesus was. The Gospel writers composed the final forms of their works with an eye toward their significance for particular communities. The gathered materials had been formulated and adapted in various settings over forty or more years. And, of course, they all sought to tell us the "honest truth" about Jesus, as best they could.

Getting Back to Jesus

Are there ways of going behind the Gospel texts and the traditions of the early church and getting back to Jesus himself? Biblical scholars have developed several tools to isolate material in the Gospels that most likely goes back to Jesus. If a teaching is unlike anything in Jewish and early Christian traditions, then it probably can be assigned directly to Jesus. An example would be Jesus' absolute prohibition of taking oaths: "Do not swear at all" (Matthew 5:34).

Other such criteria include: when a tradition appears in several different sources (Last Supper); local Palestinian coloring (Aramaic words, Palestinian farming methods); embarrassment at what might reflect badly on Jesus (his reception of John's "baptism of repentance for the forgiveness of sins," see Mark 1:4); what led to Jesus' death (the "cleansing" of the temple); and coherence (what fits with what can be established by other criteria).

These historical methods do not tell us everything we would like to know about Jesus. Nor do they necessarily establish what was most important about him.

But they do tell us something.

Jesus' Ministry

Study of the Gospels and application of these historical criteria make it possible to develop an outline of Jesus' public career. Having been raised in Nazareth in Galilee, Jesus accepted baptism from John and may have been a member of John's movement.

When Jesus went out on his own to continue and adapt John's mission, he gathered disciples near the Sea of Galilee at Capernaum, including some of John's followers. He spent much of his public life preaching about the kingdom of God and how to prepare for it. He also healed the sick as a sign of the presence of God's kingdom.

Before Passover in the spring of AD 30, Jesus and his followers made a long journey to Jerusalem. There he continued his ministry of teaching and healing but ran into intense opposition from some other Jews (especially the temple officials and scribes) and from the Roman authorities. Under the Roman prefect, Pontius Pilate, Jesus was executed by crucifixion as a rebel and a religious troublemaker. Also, he was said to have appeared alive again to some of his followers.

Careful study of the Gospels also allows us to reconstruct the major themes in Jesus' teaching. At the center was the reign or kingdom of God in both its present and future dimensions. Jesus' relationship to God was so close that he addressed God as "Father" and invited others to do the same. He proclaimed the possibility of the forgiveness of sins and of reconciliation with God.

Jesus challenged his followers to love their enemies and told them how to act in anticipation of the coming kingdom of God. He showed special concern for marginal persons—the poor, the lame, "sinners and tax collectors," prostitutes and so on—and manifested a free attitude toward the traditions associated with the Jewish Law and the Jerusalem temple. Most of these themes appear in the Lord's Prayer that Jesus taught to his disciples.

Historical Quest

The Jesus whom modern historians can recover and investigate by using the tools of historical research is sometimes called the "historical Jesus." A more accurate term would be the "historian's Jesus." This Jesus is not the whole person of Jesus, nor is he the traditional object of Christian faith.

The one whom we worship is not only the earthly Jesus but also, and especially, the risen Jesus who will come again in glory. Christians believe that there is a close continuity between the earthly Jesus and the Christ of faith and that the two cannot be totally separated.

The quest for the historical Jesus, however, refers to the project of separating the earthly Jesus from the Christ of faith. It began among liberal German Protestants in the late eighteenth century in an effort to peel away the wrappings given to Jesus in church tradition and to recover the simple figure of the "real" Jesus.

Many of the early seekers discarded the miracles of Jesus and rejected his virginal conception and resurrection as "unhistorical." One positive development in the nineteenth century was the recognition of the kingdom of God as the focus of Jesus' teaching and its roots in Jewish hopes about God's future actions on behalf of his people (sometimes called "eschatology" or "apocalyptic").

The quest in the twentieth century focused on the parables of Jesus as a way of recovering the "voice" of Jesus about the kingdom, developing criteria for identifying material from Jesus and situating

Jesus within Judaism. Recent presentations of Jesus have depicted him as a prophet sent to speak of the end times, a wisdom teacher, a philosopher and a poet skilled in his use of parables and images.

Meaning for Today

While charged with frustration, the quest for the historical Jesus has been a fascinating and even irresistible topic. It reminds us that there is no uninterpreted Jesus and that we are dependent on sources that historians find challenging.

For people of faith, the witness of the Gospels is more important than the historian's Jesus. Nevertheless, historical methods can help us to see the basic reliability of the tradition about Jesus and to encounter Jesus as the strong personality behind the Gospels and the traditions and truths contained in them.

.   .   .   .

THE "OTHER" GOSPELS

Many scholars believe that Mark's Gospel was completed around AD 70. A decade or so later Matthew and Luke used it as a source for their Gospels. They may have had another source in common, known as Q (from the German word *Quelle*, "source"), as well as their own separate sources. Q was most likely a collection of Jesus' sayings, but with none of the miracle stories so familiar to us, and no accounts of Jesus' passion.

The Gospel of Thomas is a "sayings gospel" written perhaps as late as the second century. Even though it contains many of the same parables and sayings as the Gospels of Matthew, Mark, Luke and John, the church does not consider it to be authentic revelation because it was not in widespread use among the early Christian communities.

Other texts not included in the Bible contain folktales about the life of the boy Jesus or the childhood of Mary. The best known are the *Infancy Gospel of Thomas* and the *Infancy Gospel of James*. They contain fanciful tales such as Jesus making clay pigeons and clapping his hands to bring them to life or getting mad at a playmate, causing the child's death by an angry word and then raising him to life again. While these stories may be appealing, their authenticity is questionable.

. . . .

QUESTIONS

• Who is Jesus to you? How does what you know about him affect your relationship with him? Can growing in knowledge of Jesus help you grow in love for him?

• How much are you swayed by the images of Jesus presented by recent books and movies that are based on nonbiblical sources about Jesus? Do these sources challenge or strengthen your faith?

• The four Gospels are the major sources for what we know about Jesus. Choose one of the Gospels and read it from beginning to end. What characteristics of Jesus does it emphasize?

CHAPTER TWO

· *The World of Jesus* ·

T he Incarnation of the Word of God took place in the land of
Israel (also known as Palestine) two thousand years ago. This
includes the same geographical area we hear and read about in the
daily news from the Middle East: Jerusalem, Bethlehem, Galilee, the
West Bank. Jesus lived his entire life in this part of the world.

Because of Jesus' presence and that of many other biblical figures, this area is often referred to as the "Holy Land." Those who visit
the Holy Land will inevitably hear it described as "the fifth gospel."
Such a visit can contribute greatly to one's appreciation of Jesus as a
historical figure and a Jew.

Setting the Stage

The Holy Land is relatively small, about the size of Massachusetts or
New Jersey. The northern area, with the Sea of Galilee and the
Jordan River at its eastern border, is called Galilee; this was Jesus'
home for most of his life. The central portion is Samaria, and the

southern section is known as Judea. The capital of Judea and the center of Jewish religious practice in Jesus' time was Jerusalem, the place where Jesus was put to death.

During Jesus' adult life, Galilee was ruled by Herod Antipas, one of the sons of Herod the Great. Judea was overseen directly by the Roman prefect or governor, Pontius Pilate, between AD 26 and 36. It was in this geographical and historical context that Jesus lived and worked. The Romans served as protectors for the Judeans from the mid–second century BC onward. However, by the first century AD they had integrated Palestine into their own empire and taken direct political control of Judea.

Jesus' Birth

The major sources about Jesus' birth and upbringing are the infancy narratives in Matthew 1—2 and Luke 1—2. Because they combine historical facts, biblical interpretations and theology, they are especially challenging for modern historians.

A special difficulty is posed by the evangelists' independent references to the virginal conception of Jesus. It is clear that Mary of Nazareth was the mother of Jesus, and her husband Joseph was the legal father of Jesus. But according to the Gospels of Matthew and Luke, the child Jesus was conceived "from the Holy Spirit." The rules of strict modern historical scholarship do not allow for divine interventions in human affairs or for unique cases. But the Gospels present Jesus both as a divine being and as unique among humankind.

Historians today often try to explain away the virginal conception of Jesus as an example of the "birth of the hero" myth or as a cover story for Jesus' illegitimate birth. But the parallels from other ancient texts are not convincing, and the rumors of Jesus' illegitimacy more likely reflect early Christian affirmations of his virginal conception and hostile reactions to them. So we are left with the fact that the only ancient sources we have independently state that Jesus was miraculously conceived through the power of the Holy Spirit.

Matthew and Luke also agree that Jesus was born in Bethlehem, near Jerusalem. Matthew gives the impression that Mary and Joseph had been living there already, while Luke explains that they traveled from Nazareth to Bethlehem so that Joseph, as a descendant of David, could be registered in his ancestral home as part of a Roman census.

The place of Jesus' birth contributes to his identity as the Messiah (Matthew 2:6) and as the Son of David. While some historians consider this to be all too neat and even possibly invented for theological purposes, again the only ancient sources we have agree independently that Jesus was born in the town of Bethlehem.

Jesus' Family

According to Mark 6:3 and Matthew 13:55–56, Jesus had four "brothers" named James, Joses (or Joseph), Judas and Simon, as well as several "sisters." Since the second and third centuries these "brothers" and "sisters" have been explained in various ways—as full siblings of Jesus, as Joseph's children from an earlier marriage or as relatives (possibly cousins) who lived in the same area. The first explanation conflicts with the church's tradition about Mary's perpetual virginity, while the other two do not.

No one doubts that Jesus was raised in Nazareth in Galilee. That town did not have a distinguished history. We get a hint of this in John's Gospel when Nathanael, one of Jesus' first disciples, asked, "Can anything good come out of Nazareth?" (1:46).

According to Mark, Jesus worked as a *tekton*, usually translated as "carpenter" but probably meaning something broader like a general construction worker whose skills included carpentry. Matthew states that Jesus was the son of a carpenter. Both Joseph and Jesus may have worked on the elaborate buildings recently excavated at Sepphoris, not far from Nazareth.

Jesus, the Jew

Luke's infancy narrative affirms that Jesus had a traditional Jewish upbringing. He was circumcised and named on the eighth day after his birth. Forty days after his birth he was "presented" at the Jerusalem temple in keeping with the Jewish Law. At the age of twelve he made a Passover pilgrimage to the temple with his parents. John's Gospel indicates that Jesus made other pilgrimages as an adult in addition to the final pilgrimage that led to his death.

That Jesus participated in worship at the synagogue in Nazareth is clear from several Gospel accounts. Mark, Matthew and Luke portray him as reading the Scriptures in public and teaching there. The embarrassing fact that the people of his hometown rejected him serves as a guarantee of the event's historical foundation. This is not the kind of story that early Christians might invent.

First-Century Judaism

Jews in Jesus' time were united by three great institutions: the Jerusalem temple, the land of Israel and the Law of Moses. Within that framework there were several different ways of being a Jew.

• The *Pharisees* were a lay movement that sought to extend the temple purity rules to all Jews and emphasized common meals featuring religious discussion.

• The *Sadducees* were a more conservative group that by Jesus' time had gained influence over the temple and its priesthood.

• The *Essenes* stressed community life and asceticism. Likely they were the people behind the Dead Sea Scrolls. These were ancient manuscripts discovered in the late 1940s that were the remnants of the library of a Jewish religious sect usually identified as the Essenes.

• The *Zealots* were an activist group that engaged in armed resistance against the Roman occupiers and Jewish collaborators.

• There were also end-time visionaries, scribes, chief priests, tax collectors and "sinners" (Jews who by choice or occupation, such as pig-keeping, did not observe all of the Jewish Law).

DANIEL J. HARRINGTON, S.J.

Jesus' Place in Judaism

Where does Jesus fit on this map of Jewish groups and movements? On the one hand, Jesus has been described as a "marginal Jew" in a book of the same name by John P. Meier on the grounds that he defies any specific categorization.[2] On the other hand, the scholar N.T. Wright portrays him in *Jesus and the Victory of God* as the incarnation of his people Israel and all its hopes.[3]

We can say with some confidence that Jesus lived as an observant Jew; his quarrel was with the traditions attached to the Law. We can also say that among the various Jewish groups he was closest to the Pharisees in that they shared interest in such topics as resurrection, Sabbath observance and the relative importance of ritual purity and entered into debate with them. What is beyond any doubt is that Jesus had some connection with the movement begun by John the Baptist.

The Ministry of John the Baptist

According to Luke's infancy narrative, John was born to Zechariah and Elizabeth in their old age, and was a relative of Jesus through Mary. Luke notes that when John grew up "he was in the wilderness" (1:80) before he began his public ministry. That wilderness would have been the Judean desert, where the Dead Sea Scrolls were discovered in 1947. If there is any direct connection between Jesus and the Dead Sea Scrolls, it would most likely have come about through John the Baptist.

The Jewish historian Flavius Josephus provides a brief description of John the Baptist in his *Jewish Antiquities*, in a passage not modified by Christian scribes. Josephus describes John as "a good man"[4] who urged his fellow Jews to practice virtue, to act justly and to show piety toward God. He also referred to John's distinctive rite of baptism in connection with repentance and forgiveness of sins. He attributed John's execution under Herod Antipas to Herod's fear that John's growing popularity might result in some kind of rebellion.

17

According to the Gospels, John proclaimed the coming kingdom of God in connection with his rite of baptism. Receiving John's baptism was a sign of one's willingness to turn one's life around and to prepare for the divine judgment that will accompany the full coming of God's kingdom.

Jesus and John

That Jesus underwent John's baptism is another well-established fact. Since John's baptism was associated with "repentance for the forgiveness of sins," (Mark 1:4; Luke 3:3) this was not something that early Christians would have created.

It is also likely that John the Baptist served as a mentor to Jesus, one who to some extent guided Jesus, especially with regard to his vision of the coming kingdom and how to prepare for it.

Eventually Jesus went his own way. Whereas John adopted an ascetic and world-denying lifestyle, Jesus celebrated festive meals and preached to all kinds of people. Whereas John emphasized the future coming of God's kingdom, Jesus also stressed its present dimensions. And whereas John preached moral renewal as a way to get ready for God's judgment, Jesus invited sinners to throw themselves on the grace and mercy of God.

John's Followers Become Jesus' Disciples

In John's Gospel we read that the first two disciples of Jesus came to him on the recommendation of John the Baptist from within his own circle of followers (1:35–42). When he saw Jesus walk by, John said, "Look, here is the Lamb of God" (1:36). One of the two disciples was Andrew, who then brought his brother, Simon Peter, to Jesus.

Mark tells a somewhat different story. Simon and Andrew encounter Jesus while doing their work as commercial fishermen by the Sea of Galilee. When Jesus says to them, "Follow me and I will make you fish for people," they immediately drop everything and go with him (1:16–18).

While prospective Jewish students usually sought out a teacher, here the teacher calls the prospective students and they come. The lack of prior contact and preparation makes the story all the more dramatic. The reader naturally wonders why these businessmen would give up their livelihood and family lives to join in the mission of Jesus merely on the strength of his command "Follow me." Mark's version thus highlights the personal charisma of Jesus.

Jesus' first followers eventually became part of the group of the twelve, the inner circle among Jesus' disciples and the symbol of the renewed Israel (recalling the twelve tribes of ancient Israel). It was their privilege to be with Jesus and to share in his mission and ministry. Although the first disciples often misunderstood Jesus and even fled when he was arrested, they provided continuity between the public activity of the earthly Jesus and the formation of the early church.

On the historical level there is very likely something to the connection between the disciples of John the Baptist and the first followers of Jesus. It is also likely that Jesus' first followers already shared something of his hope for and dedication to the kingdom of God. They may first have learned this from John the Baptist.

THE HOLY LAND

The Holy Land is held sacred by the three religions that trace their roots to Abraham: Judaism, Christianity and Islam. God promised this land to Abraham when he called him to leave his homeland. Jews are descended from Isaac, the son of God's promise to Abraham and Sarah. According to the Qur'an Muslims are descended from Ishmael, Abraham's son through Hagar. Moses led the people of Israel into this Promised Land when they were freed from slavery in Egypt. Christians revere it as the place where Jesus the Christ was born into the ancient royal family of the Hebrew King David and where he lived, died and rose from the dead.

Although we know it as the birthplace of the Prince of Peace, the Holy Land has known little peace in its long history. In the ancient world it had military and economic value because it provided a land link from Egypt to Syria and Mesopotamia when the only alternative was crossing the Arabian Desert. One ancient superpower after another—Assyria, Babylon, Persia, Greece, Rome—attempted to conquer this strip of land known as the Fertile Crescent. In the Middle Ages the Crusades pitted Christians against Muslims for control of Jerusalem and surrounding areas. Even today the Holy Land is at the heart of some of the most bitter territory disputes in the world.

. . . .

QUESTIONS

- Jesus was a first-century Jew from the Middle East. Does your image of Jesus reflect this ethnicity of Jesus? What has influenced your image of Jesus?

- Jesus was from a common family, a no-name town and a people who were "God's chosen" yet subject to the rule of others. What does this say to you about how you live your life and where you have placed your priorities?

- John the Baptist preached repentance. Jesus called his first disciples with the words "Follow me." How is repentance (or lack of it) affecting your ability to follow Jesus?

CHAPTER THREE

· *Jesus and the Kingdom* ·

When Matthew sat down to summarize the preaching of John the Baptist early in his Gospel, he wrote: "Repent, for the kingdom of heaven has come near" (3:2).

The first words that Matthew attributed to Jesus as he began his public ministry are exactly the same: "Repent, for the kingdom of heaven has come near" (4:17). The kingdom of God was the central theme in the preaching of both John the Baptist and Jesus. (The "kingdom of heaven" was Matthew's typically Jewish substitute expression. As a sign of reverence Jews avoided using the name of God.)

Thy Kingdom Come
In the context of first-century Judaism, the "kingdom of God" referred especially to God's future display of power and judgment and to the final establishment of God's rule over all creation. Then, all people and all creation will recognize and acknowledge the God

of Israel as the only God and Lord. This is what we ask for when we pray: "Thy kingdom come!"

When the day of the Lord comes and God's kingdom is fully established, the will of God shall be done on earth as it is in heaven. Jesus' own prayer—the Lord's Prayer—is, first and foremost, a prayer for the coming of God's kingdom in its fullness.

The theme of the kingdom of God dates to the Old Testament, where we read about God's eternal kingship and the monarchy in ancient Israel. Many of the "kingship" psalms of the Hebrew Bible begin by celebrating Yahweh, the God of Israel, as king over all creation: "The LORD is king!" (Psalms 93:1; 97:1; 99:1).

God's kingly rule was revealed especially in Israel's exodus from Egypt, and that rule is also associated with God's justice and judgment: "The LORD is king! / The world is firmly established; it shall never be moved. / He will judge the peoples with equity" (Psalm 96:10).

In the debate about anointing Saul as king over Israel, the chief hesitation concerned the relationship of the earthly king to the kingship of God: "they [Israel] have rejected me [God] from being king over them" (1 Samuel 8:7).

From Present to Future Fulfillment

From the sixth century BC onward, after Israel's exile to Babylon and its return, the emphasis on God's kingship shifted from the present to the future. The people were oppressed, in turn, by the Persians, the Greeks and the Romans. It became increasingly difficult for them to imagine how God's promise of an eternal kingship from the line of David could ever be fulfilled under such conditions.

One possibility of this fulfillment was that in the "last days" of the present age in human history, God's kingship would be made evident in a truly spectacular way. Then the righteous in Israel would be vindicated and granted what had been promised to God's people.

In describing the future manifestation of God's reign, the Jewish writers of the day used words and images from earlier times: the day of the Lord, the divine warrior, God as king, the anointed one (Messiah), cosmic signs and so forth. But they placed these words and images in a new context that pointed to the last days (eschatological) or the future (apocalyptic).

Justice Will Prevail

In Jewish writings of Jesus' time there was no uniform description of the events accompanying the full coming of God's kingdom.

• Daniel writes of a cosmic battle featuring the archangel Michael, the great tribulation and the vindication of the righteous and wise in their resurrection to eternal life (see 12:1–3).

• In 1 Enoch (a Jewish apocalyptic book containing writings from the third century BC to the first century AD), we learn that there will be the establishment of justice in Israel, a judgment upon the whole world and a new heaven and a new earth (see 91:12–17).

• The Assumption of Moses, another early Jewish apocalyptic writing, foresees cosmic signs accompanying the coming of the kingdom as well as punishments for the gentiles and exaltation for Israel (see 10:1–10).

• The Rule of the Community, one of the Dead Sea Scrolls, contains regulations and related materials for Jewish life in something like a monastery. While affirming God's ultimate sovereignty, it describes the present age as under two powers (the Prince of Light and the Angel of Darkness) and looks forward to a decisive divine visitation or intervention that will usher in the fullness of God's reign (see 3:13—4:26).

Underlying all these scenarios is the conviction that when the course of history has been accomplished, God will vindicate Israel (or the faithful within it) by destroying evil and evildoers, and by bringing about a new heaven and a new earth where goodness and justice will prevail. It is God's task to fulfill his promises to Israel and to establish the kingdom for all creation to see and celebrate.

Jesus Preaches the Future Kingdom

That Jesus shared the hopes of his Jewish contemporaries for the future coming of God's kingdom is indicated by the summary of his preaching in Matthew 4:17 ("Repent, for the kingdom of heaven has come near") and by the Lord's Prayer ("Thy kingdom come, thy will be done on earth as it is in heaven," see Matthew 6:10; Luke 11:2). We can learn even more from the parables, which many scholars agree best represent the "voice" of the historical Jesus regarding the kingdom of God.

Matthew 13 contains several short parables that begin with the words "The kingdom of heaven is like...". The twin parables of the mustard seed and the yeast (13:31–33) emphasize that the kingdom's small beginnings in the present (especially in Jesus' own preaching) will produce great results as symbolized by the large mustard bush and the abundance of bread.

The twin parables of the hidden treasure and the precious pearl (13:44–46) stress the extraordinary value of the coming kingdom and the total commitment that it deserves and demands. The parables of the wheat and weeds (13:24–30, 36–43) and the fishing net (13:47–50) indicate that the full coming of God's kingdom will be accompanied by a divine judgment that will separate the good from the bad and give them their appropriate rewards and punishments.

These parables, and many other passages in the New Testament, affirm that there will be a clear and more obvious manifestation of God's rule in the future. It will include a divine judgment in which the righteous will be vindicated and the wicked will be condemned.

Future—and Present

While the "kingdom of heaven" parables in Matthew 13 look to the future, they also have a present dimension. The kingdom is present now, even if in a small way, in the mustard seed, the yeast, the hidden treasure and the pearl.

Moreover, something important pertaining to the kingdom is going on now: The mustard seed is growing into a great bush; the yeast is expanding the flour; and the treasure and the pearl are present realities insofar as they can be found, handled and enjoyed here and now. While Jesus shared the hopes of his contemporaries for the fullness of God's kingdom, he also wanted to alert people to the presence of God's kingdom already among them.

Jesus' Words Confirm the Kingdom as Present

Three sayings in the Gospels of Matthew and Luke confirm that God's kingdom is a present entity. All of these sayings reflect with a very high degree of probability the views of the historical Jesus.

• In Luke 11:20 (and Matthew 12:28), Jesus defends his practice of casting out demons by saying: "But if it is by the finger of God that I cast out the demons, then the kingdom of God has come to you." The "finger of God" alludes to Old Testament contests between Pharaoh's magicians and Moses the miracle worker (see Exodus 8:19). The Gospel saying claims that Jesus' healings and exorcisms are present manifestations of God's reign and represent his victory over demonic forces.

• In Matthew 11:12 (and Luke 16:16), Jesus says: "From the days of John the Baptist until now the kingdom of heaven has suffered violence, and the violent take it by force." The idea is that from John to Jesus, the kingdom of God was real enough in the present to have been the object of violent opposition. Surely Jesus alludes to John's execution under Herod Antipas. Moreover, the opposition that Jesus himself faced was another sign that the kingdom was present in his ministry.

• In Luke 17:21, Jesus tells the Pharisees: "the kingdom of God is among you." Jesus here rejects the idea that the kingdom will come only with cosmic signs, and reminds his audience that the kingdom is to some extent already present. The translations "among you" and "in your midst" are preferable to "within you." (The familiar rendering "within you" involves an excessively individual and spiritual interpretation that would be foreign to the first-century Jewish context.)

These three sayings are widely regarded as expressing the "voice" of the historical Jesus about the kingdom of God. They all suggest that, according to Jesus, the kingdom of God has a present dimension as well as future dimensions. These sayings assert that Jesus' healings and other miracles were present signs of the kingdom, that the kingdom was enough of a present reality to suffer violent opposition and that the kingdom is "among us" and "in our midst" if only we look hard enough for it.

Jesus Embodies the Kingdom

The parables and sayings tell us that God's kingdom was present in the person and ministry of Jesus in an especially powerful way. The early Christian writer Origen described Jesus as "the kingdom itself."[5] In other words, Jesus was the embodiment or Incarnation of the kingdom of God.

One of the puzzles that some New Testament scholars have found especially difficult to explain is why, in the Gospels of Matthew, Mark and Luke, the focus is on the kingdom of God, while in John's Gospel the focus is on Jesus himself as the revealer and revelation of God. The answer may be found in the idea of Jesus as "the kingdom itself," as the present manifestation of the kingdom of God par excellence.

Goal and Horizon of Christian Living

The theme of the kingdom of God offers the goal and the horizon for Christian life. The fullness of the kingdom remains beyond human comprehension and control. It is God's task and privilege to bring it about in God's own time. The Resurrection of Jesus is the most dramatic and significant anticipation of the fullness of God's kingdom, since in Jewish thought resurrection was understood to be a collective event in the future that would serve as a prelude to the Last Judgment.

The other teachings of Jesus are always set in the framework of the kingdom of God. The three great questions of human existence are: Who am I? What is my goal in life? How do I get there? For followers of Jesus, the goal is the kingdom of God. Those who aspire to fullness of life in God's kingdom follow the teachings and example of Jesus. In this way they may enter the kingdom of God.

The kingdom of God was the central theme in Jesus' life and teaching. He is well described as the prophet of God's kingdom. While he shared hopes for the coming kingdom with his Jewish contemporaries, he also insisted that the kingdom of God is among us and in our midst. He was not only the perfect embodiment of his own teaching, but he also provided for his followers a sound framework for living in the present so that they, too, might enter that kingdom.

. . . .

KINGDOM OF PEACE

David, Israel's greatest king, was renowned as a military leader. He first came to the attention of the royal court when he single-handedly defeated the Philistine giant Goliath with a slingshot—and unwavering faith in God.

At the time of Jesus, most people expected that the long-awaited Messiah would be a military leader like David. The country was under Roman occupation, and small groups of Zealots and rebels would rise up in armed resistance. This strategy, notably used by the Maccabees, was at times successful in throwing off foreign domination.

When Jesus came preaching a message of peace and a non-military basis for the kingdom of God, it surprised and even dismayed many of his followers. The Gospels tell us that even his closest disciples questioned him on several occasions about when he was going to restore rule to Israel. It wasn't until he triumphed over death itself, a far greater foe than the Romans, that they realized the Messiah's true identity. Jesus fulfilled the promise of the Hebrew prophets. They had urged the people and leaders to put their faith in God and not in human might. Like David's boyhood dismissal of Saul's armor and weaponry in order to rely solely on God, Jesus' strength as the Messiah came from the Lord alone.

.   .   .   .

QUESTIONS

- Where do you see the kingdom of God present in the world today? Which parable about the kingdom means the most to you? Why do you think that is?

- When you pray the words "thy kingdom come" in the Lord's Prayer, what are you praying for? How would you explain the kingdom of God to a young child?

- What are you doing to be a servant of the kingdom so that one day it will be fully realized? What about your faith community? Are you—and it—being called to do more?

CHAPTER FOUR

• *Jesus the Teacher* •

The kingdom of God was the heart of Jesus' teaching. He focused on both the present and the future dimensions of God's kingdom. He tried to convey a vision of the present world as radiating the glory and the power of God. Jesus sought also to provide reasons for hope about the future as he taught people to look forward to and pray for the full coming of God's reign. Jesus was the prophet of God's kingdom.

As a prophet Jesus was also a teacher. He was a wise teacher, and so he used the methods that wise teachers use. His primary audience was made up of ordinary people who lived in first-century Galilee. For them he had a message of hope.

Teaching With Parables

Jesus tried to meet his listeners in their own lives and to use their ordinary experiences as tools to help them better understand the kingdom. For farmers he used illustrations from farming. For fishermen he took images from fishing. For homemakers he told stories pertaining to their everyday lives, which included cooking and housecleaning.

Jesus addressed people in their own settings. But his goal was always to give them glimpses of the kingdom of God. He wanted to show them how to discern the kingdom's present dimensions as well as prepare for eternal life with God in its fullness.

Though Jesus was an effective teacher, the main focus of his teachings—the kingdom of God—presented challenges. How does one talk about something beyond human comprehension and control? It is God's kingdom, and not ours, to give. Its fullness belongs to the future, the last days. Its present dimensions are signs of its future fullness. The best is yet to come.

Jesus frequently used parables in teaching about God's kingdom. The word *parable* derives from the Greek verb *paraballo*, which means "to place one thing beside another." A parable is a form of analogy that seeks to illuminate one reality by appealing to something better known.

A parable may be defined as a story, taken from nature or everyday life, about an interesting or unusual case, which points to another level or topic and teases the mind of the listener into active thinking. We'll look at parables in Matthew 13 to demonstrate.

The Power of a Good Story

Almost everyone enjoys stories. Children often say, "Tell me a story." A story takes us out of ourselves, at least for a moment, and transports us into a new and different setting. It engages our imagination and makes us eager to find out how the story will end. The parables in Matthew 13 are, first of all, stories. They concern a farmer who sows seeds, a small amount of yeast, a tiny mustard seed, wheat and weeds sown together in a field, buried treasure, a precious pearl and fishermen casting their dragnets.

These parables reflect aspects of nature and everyday life in first-century Galilee, where farming and fishing were major occupations. However, in each parable something unusual surfaces: a miraculously big harvest, a large mustard bush, a huge amount of bread, a mixed harvest that needs sorting, precious goods discovered by accident and a catch of fish that needs to be separated.

More Than a Typical Story

The deeper level to which each parable points is announced at the beginning of all but the parable of the sower: "The kingdom of heaven is like...." We are told from the start that these short stories are intended to teach us something about the kingdom of God. And the purpose of these parables is to make us ask questions and think about that kingdom. At each point we are led to ask: What aspect of the kingdom does this little story bring out?

Scholars generally agree that the parables allow us to hear the "voice" of the historical Jesus. They reflect life in first-century Galilee, where Jesus lived and worked, where farming and fishing were common occupations. They manifest a certain coherence of thought and convey a consistent vision of the present and future dimensions of the kingdom of God.

In the Gospels Jesus never defined the kingdom of God. Nor did he ever provide a theological treatise on the topic. Instead, he communicated his vision of the kingdom through short stories and images well suited to his first audiences in Galilee. He taught in a way that engaged the imaginations of his hearers, and he invited them to think about various aspects of God's kingdom. His focus on the kingdom gave his listeners—and gives us—a goal to strive for and a horizon against which to live and act.

Prophet or Wisdom Teacher?

Jesus used many of the literary techniques and rhetorical devices that other Jewish wisdom teachers of his day employed to convey their visions of God and of human existence. In recent years scholars have been divided over whether Jesus should be classified as a prophet pointing to the last days or as a wisdom teacher. But this is a false contrast. The wisdom writings discovered in 1947 among the Dead Sea Scrolls at Qumran (see the appendix) have confirmed that there was no sharp division between hope for God's coming kingdom and the literary forms and concerns of Jewish wisdom teachers.

The kingdom of God was the goal and horizon of Jesus' teaching. Jesus wanted to help people to enter the kingdom of God and enjoy its fullness. Much of his "ethical" teaching concerned the values and virtues most appropriate for those seeking to enter the kingdom. He sought to show people how to reach their goal of eternal happiness with God.

The "Sermon" of Jesus

The Sermon on the Mount (Matthew 5—7) is a summary of Jesus' teachings. Rather than the transcript of a speech delivered in one place at one time, it is more likely a collection of Jesus' sayings taken from several different sources and assembled by the evangelist Matthew or a predecessor. Nevertheless, its individual sayings reflect with a high degree of probability the actual teachings of the historical Jesus. They allow us to hear the "voice" of Jesus.

The Sermon begins with a series of beatitudes in which Jesus declares some unlikely persons to be happy or fortunate: "Blessed are the poor in spirit, for theirs is the kingdom of heaven." "Blessed are those who hunger and thirst for righteousness, for they will be filled." "Blessed are the merciful, for they will receive mercy." They are followed by analogies that declare Jesus' followers to be "the salt of the earth" and "the light of the world." Then, in an "I" saying, Jesus declares, "Do not think that I have come to abolish the law or the prophets; I have come not to abolish but to fulfill." This is followed by six contrasts or antitheses: "You have heard that it was said.... But I say to you..." (Matthew 5:3, 6, 7, 13, 14, 17; see also 21–48).

In the next section (6:1–18) Jesus lays down rules regarding three practices of piety: almsgiving, prayer and fasting. He provides the Lord's Prayer as a sample prayer. In 6:19—7:12 he gives instructions concerning various topics in no particular order, a format found in other biblical wisdom books (Proverbs, Ecclesiastes, Sirach). Within this block of teachings there are prohibitions ("Do not store up for yourselves treasures on earth," 6:19), sayings ("No one can serve two masters," 6:24) and the "golden rule" ("[D]o to others as you would have them do to you," 7:12). Verses 7:13–27 end the Sermon with cautions about the need to put Jesus' challenging teachings into practice ("Beware of false prophets, who come to you in sheep's clothing," 7:15). All these different literary devices in the Sermon on the Mount show that Jesus was a wisdom teacher in the service of the kingdom of God.

Guidelines for Aspirants to the Kingdom

The Sermon on the Mount provides a sample of the content of Jesus' ethical teaching. With the kingdom of God as the goal and horizon, the specific teachings are intended as directives or guidelines toward reaching that goal. Jesus is the instructor, and his Sermon can be aptly described as a wisdom instruction such as one finds especially in Proverbs and Sirach.

The Beatitudes offer a sketch of character traits, attitudes and virtues that are fitting for those seeking the kingdom of God. As "the salt of the earth" and "the light of the world," such persons perform a vital function for and in our lives. Rather than abolishing the Law and the prophets, Jesus urges his followers to go to the roots of the individual biblical commandments and so avoid breaking even the letter of the law.

In matters of religious observance Jesus challenges his followers to examine their motivations. Almsgiving, prayer and fasting, while good in themselves, must be undertaken as ways of honoring God and not simply as means of establishing a public reputation for holiness. The various teachings in Matthew 6:19—7:12 highlight the need to seek "treasure in heaven," to serve God as one's only master, to avoid fruitless anxieties and harshly negative judgments about others, to persist in prayer and to observe the "golden rule."

Jesus' concluding challenges emphasize that the way to God's kingdom may seem hard and narrow and that his teachings demand practical application. The content of the Sermon—like the entire Gospel tradition—concerns Jesus' identity as a wisdom teacher in the service of the kingdom of God.

Teaching Through Debates and Symbolic Actions

Another common teaching form that very likely reflects the practice of the historical Jesus is the controversy or conflict story. These are short narratives (for example, Matthew 9:14–17) in which someone, often with hostile intent, approaches Jesus with a hard question ("Why do...the Pharisees fast often, but your disciples do not fast?"). The tense situation provides Jesus with an opportunity to deliver his own wise teaching, to display his superior wisdom and to escape the trap set for him by opponents. Other examples can be found in Matthew 22:15–46 where Jesus debates about paying taxes to Caesar, the resurrection, the greatest commandment in the Law and the identity of David's son.

In addition to parables, wisdom sayings and controversies, Jesus taught by symbolic actions. These passages are sometimes called *enacted parables* because they convey teaching through an activity rather than by words alone. In doing so, Jesus followed the examples of the great prophets of the Old Testament: Isaiah, Jeremiah, Ezekiel and Hosea. His actions were similar to the symbolic demonstrations used effectively by twentieth-century leaders like Gandhi and Martin Luther King, Jr.

The most striking examples of Jesus' teaching by means of symbolic actions were his "triumphal" entry into Jerusalem (Mark 11:1–11) and his "cleansing" of the temple (Mark 11:15–19). On Palm Sunday Jesus concluded his journey to Jerusalem by riding a colt and enacting the role of the humble messiah-king prophesied in Zechariah 9. Likewise, by cleansing the temple area of its excessively commercial aspects, Jesus echoed the prophetic teachings of Isaiah 56:7 ("My house shall be called a house of prayer for all the nations") and Jeremiah 7:11 (the temple as "a den of robbers") in Mark 11:17.

By such symbolic actions, Jesus confirmed his identity as the prophet of God's kingdom, one who stood in the same line as Israel's great prophets of the past and at the same time fulfilled their prophecies.

D I D   J E S U S   R E A L L Y   S A Y   I T ?

A group of scholars known as the Jesus Seminar has been meeting since 1985 to debate the authenticity of Jesus' words and actions as recorded in the Gospels. Founded by the late Robert Funk in Berkeley, California, this group has generated much controversy. In their first project the members voted on which of the sayings in the Gospels they believed could be authentically attributed to Jesus. They assigned different rankings to each saying of Jesus: certainly (red), probably (pink), probably not (gray) and certainly not (black). To people familiar with Bibles in which all the sayings of Jesus are highlighted in red, this seems blasphemous. However, few biblical scholars outside the Jesus Seminar have been convinced by the results.

Most mainline Catholic biblical scholars fall somewhere between an approach to Scripture that takes every word literally and as directly from Jesus, and the excessively skeptical approach taken by the Jesus Seminar. Translation is always an issue, since Jesus spoke Aramaic and all the Gospel manuscripts we have are in Greek. We may never know with absolute certainty which words Jesus actually spoke. But we believe that the texts of the four Gospels tell us the honest truth about Jesus, and that there is continuity between these texts, the traditions that circulated in the early church, and the voice of Jesus.

· · · · · · · · · · · · · · · · · · · ·

QUESTIONS

• What ordinary twenty-first–century images and experiences would Jesus use if he was teaching in parables today? How might they vary when used in different cultures, generations and socio-economic classes?

• What lessons can you take from Jesus concerning the ways your stories, sayings, conflicts and actions teach others about your identity and beliefs? Will this make you more conscious of your choice of words and actions?

• "The kingdom of God was the goal and horizon of Jesus' teaching." What are you doing as a servant of the kingdom to share Jesus' teaching and strive for that goal?

CHAPTER FIVE

• *Jesus the Miracle Worker* •

The evidence that Jesus was a compassionate and effective healer is overwhelming. However, this same evidence raises some difficult questions for twenty-first–century people, modern historians in particular. Do miracles really happen? Did Jesus really perform all the marvelous deeds that the Gospels report? What did those miracles mean to Jesus, the early Christians and the Gospel writers? What do they mean to us?

Jesus was a healer, not as a practitioner of medical science but rather as a miracle worker. The Gospels are full of reports about his miraculous activities. Indeed, almost one-third of Mark's Gospel is devoted to Jesus' miracles. The first half of John's Gospel contains seven miracles known as "signs" that range from Jesus turning water into wine at the wedding feast at Cana to raising his friend Lazarus from the dead. According to one estimate (counting repeated passages only once) the four Gospels include seventeen healings, six exorcisms and eight nature miracles.

The Makings of a Miracle

The common definition of *miracle* is "an event that is an exception to the laws of nature." In the Bible, however, what we call "miracles" are described more loosely as "signs and wonders" or acts of power that are attributed to God.

Moses, in the early chapters of Exodus, and the prophets Elijah and Elisha, later in the Old Testament, perform many acts of power as instruments of God. The people of ancient Israel crossing the Red Sea under Moses' leadership and crossing the Jordan River with Joshua are celebrated in the Bible as signs that God was at work in these events on behalf of his people.

New Testament scholar John P. Meier observes that a miracle has three basic components: (1) It must be an unusual event that can be perceived by others. (2) It has no natural explanation. (3) It appears to be the result of an act of God.

On Different Pages

Modern historians have a hard time with the Gospel miracle stories. These historians usually work on the following three assumptions: (1) The past is basically the same as the present. (2) Historical events can and should be interpreted only within the realm of earthly cause and effect. No supernatural interventions are allowed as explanations. (3) There are no unique historical figures.

Of course, these were not the assumptions of the evangelists or almost anyone else in antiquity, nor are they the assumptions of most people today. Meier also notes that one basic component of a miracle—interpreting the event as an act of God—goes beyond the historian's task and competence and demands a philosophical or theological judgment about the authenticity of any miracle (whether for or against).

The Gospel writers had no doubts that Jesus was a miracle worker. They all depict him performing unusual actions seen by others, for which there was no natural explanation and attribute them to the power of God made manifest in Jesus. But unlike other biblical miracle workers, Jesus acts on his own authority and power, not merely as a mediator between God and other persons.

Signs of the Kingdom

The early Christians, while acknowledging the humanity of Jesus, regarded him as a unique figure in human history—the Son of God. Nevertheless, Jesus' miracles are not so much displays of power or even proofs of his divinity as they are signs of the presence of God's kingdom in the person of Jesus. Their significance in Jesus' life and ministry is captured nicely in his own words: "If it is by the finger of God that I cast out the demons, then the kingdom of God has come to you" (Luke 11:20). This saying provides the key to a proper understanding of Jesus' miracles.

During his lifetime there was little doubt about Jesus' ability to heal and perform other types of miracles. Even his opponents acknowledged his power to perform such actions. Their question concerned the origin or source of Jesus' powers. Did his power come from God or from Satan? In response, Jesus tried to show the absurdity of their question, because his miracles were clearly signs of God's victory over Satan and the defeat of the powers of evil.

Miracles Lead to Discipleship

Matthew 8—9 offers a collection of stories about Jesus' miracles or mighty acts. His theological point is that Jesus the teacher was powerful not only in word (the Sermon on the Mount) but also in deed (the miracles collection). Matthew records three cycles of three miracles each, interrupted by teachings about following Jesus. In using this structure, Matthew is suggesting that the mighty acts of Jesus demand the response of discipleship. Focusing on these texts can help us to open up and better understand the literary, historical and theological dimensions of the miracle stories in the Gospels.

Healing Miracles

The majority of the miracle accounts Matthew presents in these two chapters are healing stories. Jesus heals a man with leprosy, the paralyzed servant of a Roman centurion, Peter's mother-in-law who was suffering from a fever, another paralyzed man, a woman with a flow of blood, two blind men and a man unable to speak.

In each case we get some minimal information about the person's medical condition, but never anything like a full diagnosis. This was not the evangelist's real interest. In most instances the sick person or a friend approaches Jesus in a spirit of faith and asks for healing. Jesus responds with words or sometimes with a touch, and the healing is immediate and complete. The narratives often end with expressions of awe on the part of the audience or with some other "proof" that a miraculous healing has taken place.

Matthew has taken these miracle stories from Mark or some other source and shaped them to bring out his favorite theme of "praying faith." His special interest in Jesus' healings was not so much in the spectacular displays of Jesus' power but rather in the prayerful encounter between persons in great need and Jesus the powerful healer.

These stories had been handed on and reshaped in the early church for many years before Matthew came to write down his Gospel near the end of the first century AD. Those who passed them on were less interested in piling up factual details than they were in exploring the significance of these stories for their lives—and our own.

"The Dead Are Raised"

The accounts about Jesus restoring dead people to life represent a special category among the healing narratives. In one such story

Jesus restores to life the daughter of a synagogue leader who tells Jesus of her death. "[B]ut come and lay your hand on her, and she will live" (Matthew 9:18).

Similar stories are told by Luke about the son of the widow of Nain and by John about Jesus' friend Lazarus. While we assume that these persons would eventually die a second time, the narratives foreshadow the Resurrection of Jesus and also are signs of the Messiah's presence among us: "the blind receive their sight, the lame walk...the dead are raised" (see Matthew 11:5; Luke 7:22; Isaiah 35:5–6).

Exorcisms

Matthew also records two exorcisms, that is, the healings of persons who were thought to be possessed by demons or by Satan, the prince of demons. One is a much shorter version of Mark's account about the Gerasene demoniac. In Matthew's version two possessed men behave aggressively toward others. But the demons within them recognize that Jesus is the Son of God and that his appearance marks the end of the time for their domination over the two men. Jesus sends the demons into a herd of pigs, who in turn jump into the Sea of Galilee and drown. Of course, pigs were unclean animals for Jews, and so the story has an element of insider ethnic humor. The second exorcism story is about a man whose inability to speak is explained in terms of demonic possession. He is healed as soon as the demon is expelled.

An exorcism account is a form of a healing story. There are other exorcisms in Mark's Gospel: the possessed man in the synagogue at Capernaum, the possessed boy and the daughter of the Syrophoenician woman. Moreover, according to Luke, Mary Magdalene ("from whom seven demons had gone out") had been healed of demonic possession, presumably by Jesus.

Expelling "Demons"

For historians the problem raised by Jesus' exorcisms is the nature of the maladies involved. Were they a sign that the persons he healed were actually taken over by demonic supernatural forces? Or were their symptoms due to conditions that psychiatrists today might diagnose as mania, depression or schizophrenia?

Was their abnormal and aggressive behavior due to the tense and repressive political situation in which they lived? To what extent are these stories imaginative representations of Jesus' victory over the forces of evil in the world? Elements from any or all of these explanations may have been factors underlying the Gospels' exorcism narratives.

Nature Miracles

There is one nature miracle in Matthew 8—9. Jesus stops a storm on the Sea of Galilee by his words alone: "[H]e got up and rebuked the winds and the sea; and there was a dead calm" (8:26). Other nature miracles in Matthew (and other Gospels) include the feedings of the five thousand and the four thousand, Jesus walking on the water, Peter finding a coin in the fish's mouth and the withering of the fig tree. John's Gospel contains accounts about the changing of water into wine at the wedding feast at Cana and the miraculous catch of fish (2:1–11; 21:1–14; see also Luke 5:1–11).

The nature miracles are presented as events in Jesus' ministry that are dramatic exceptions to the laws of nature. They sometimes meet real human needs like feeding crowds and rescuing disciples. They are among the most spectacular displays of power on Jesus' part and mark him as unique among humans and, indeed, as divine.

By performing miracles such as walking on the water and in feeding the poor among God's people, Jesus does what God does in the Old Testament. The way in which the nature miracles are narrated evokes many biblical motifs and precedents and highlights the theological dimensions of Jesus' person and actions. Even more than the healings and exorcisms, the nature miracles are vehicles of early Christian theology.

Jesus the Miracle Worker

The miracles of Jesus are a major part of the Gospel tradition. Their prominence indicates that Jesus' contemporaries—and even his enemies—acknowledged that he was a miracle worker. But the nature of our sources may not allow us to answer definitively all the questions posed by modern historians.

Early Christians were not seeking to simply recount the factual details of Jesus' marvelous actions. Rather, following the lead of Jesus himself, they found in the miracles powerful signs of the presence of the kingdom of God and testimony to Jesus as the proclaimer and embodiment of God's kingdom. Believers today follow in the tradition of these early Christians.

EXORCISM: SENSATIONAL EVENT OR SPIRITUAL HEALING?

Anyone forty or older probably recalls the controversy in the early 1970s surrounding the film *The Exorcist*, based on William Peter Blatty's novel of the same title. In 2005 moviegoers were offered *The Exorcism of Emily Rose*. Pop culture's fascination with the occult influences the way we hear Gospel accounts of Jesus performing exorcisms ("casting out demons"). We might think of exorcisms as sensational, shrouded in magic and mystery.

The first century had a much different understanding of illness, particularly psychological illness. Many conditions that would be diagnosed today as medical disorders (epilepsy is a good example) were once regarded as signs of demonic possession. On the other hand, we don't take a purely scientific and skeptical approach to the Scriptures and dismiss all of Jesus' miracles as mere metaphors.

Today the church recognizes that there is still a need for exorcisms. But these rituals are performed quietly and out of the public eye so as not to sensationalize them. Like Jesus, the church prefers that people focus on the great power of God to heal. The rite of exorcism in the *Rituale Romanum* was updated in 1999, and the role of exorcist is a special calling in the church. According to news accounts Pope John Paul II performed at least three exorcisms; Cardinal Joseph Ratzinger (now Pope Benedict XVI) was on the committee that revised the ritual.

· ·

QUESTIONS

• What experience of the miraculous power of God have you had in your own life or witnessed in the lives of others?

• What difference do the accounts of Jesus as a miracle worker have in your belief in him as the Son of God? Would it be more difficult for you to believe if he had not performed miracles? Why or why not?

• Matthew suggests that the mighty acts of Jesus demand the response of discipleship. What is your response to Jesus' actions in your life? Are you being called to do more?

CHAPTER SIX

· *Jesus and Prayer* ·

Teach us to pray." This simple request from Jesus' disciples in
Luke's Gospel expresses the desire of almost everyone with a spark
of religious faith.

Saint Paul assures us that the Holy Spirit can and does help us
in our prayer and that God the Father is eager to hear our prayers
and answer them. In prayer we lift our hearts and minds to God. We
address God directly and express our joys, sorrows, frustrations and
failures.

The Gospels provide precious material about Jesus' practice of
prayer, give the texts of his prayer for the full coming of God's kingdom and offer examples of his surprising teachings about how to
pray. Everything that the Gospels present about prayer is consistent
with what we have learned so far about Jesus as the prophet of God's
kingdom, the wise teacher and the powerful and compassionate
healer and miracle worker.

Psalms and Temple Prayer

We cannot understand Jesus and prayer without looking first at his Jewish background. Jesus learned to pray from what we call the Old Testament. The book of Psalms contains 150 songs that have shaped and expressed the religious sensibilities of God's people throughout the centuries.

The psalms include hymns praising God, thanksgivings for recoveries and rescues from danger, and laments over individual and communal sufferings. The psalms in large part were composed for and used in association with the worship services at the Jerusalem temple. Jesus and his first followers would have been familiar with many of them.

Synagogue Prayers

In Jesus' time Jews who lived outside of Jerusalem developed prayers to be used in worship services held in local synagogues. There was only one temple (at Jerusalem) where sacrifices were offered, but there were many synagogues (the word means "gathering" or "meeting") throughout Israel as well as other parts of the Mediterranean world where Jews had settled. We learn from Mark and Luke that Jesus attended services in the synagogue in his hometown of Nazareth and there read the Scriptures and commented on them.

At the heart of the Jewish synagogue service are three prayers known by the Hebrew words *Shema* ("Hear"), *Shemoneh Esreh* ("Eighteen [Benedictions]") and *Kaddish* ("Hallowed"). (1) The *Shema* is the confession of faith in God as "one." It consists of the reading or recitation of three biblical passages (Deuteronomy 6:4–5; 11:13–21; Numbers 15:37–41) along with blessings before and after them. (2) The Eighteen Benedictions are praises and petitions directed to God that ask for wisdom, forgiveness of sins, help in times of trouble and so on. (3) The *Kaddish* asks that God's name be hallowed and glorified throughout the world, and that God soon establish his kingdom in its fullness.

It is likely that Jesus knew and used these prayers or others like them. The psalms and the synagogue prayers shaped the language and theology reflected in Jesus' prayers and teachings about prayer. We can see many striking parallels in form and thought between Jesus' own prayer (the Lord's Prayer) and the *Kaddish* and Eighteen Benedictions. As an observant Jew Jesus shared his tradition's zeal for God's glory, trust that God hears all our prayers and hope that he will bring about the fullness of the kingdom.

Jesus' Practice of Prayer

Luke's Gospel is often called the "Gospel of Prayer." It contains a prayer from Jesus—what we know as the Lord's Prayer—and instructions about how to pray. Luke also portrays Jesus as praying at the decisive moments in his public ministry. We learn that Jesus had a rich prayer life focused on God as his (and our) Father and that Jesus marked the most important moments in his life by turning to his Father in prayer.

If you want to know what Luke regarded as the most important moments in Jesus' life, look at his mentions of Jesus at prayer. Between Jesus' baptism and the descent of the Holy Spirit upon him, Jesus was at prayer. After his first miraculous healings, Jesus withdrew to a deserted place to pray. Before choosing the twelve apostles, Jesus spent the night in prayer. Prior to Peter's confession of Jesus as the Messiah, Jesus was at prayer.

Before the Transfiguration when the disciples received a glimpse of the glory of the risen Jesus, we are told that he went up the mountain to pray. After the Last Supper and before his arrest, he went with his disciples to the Mount of Olives to pray. And, at the moment of his death, Jesus prayed to his Father in the words of Psalm 31:5: "Father, into your hands I commend my spirit" (Luke 23:46).

In other Gospels Jesus shows himself to be rooted in the prayer traditions of his people. In Matthew he praises his Father by using the typical Jewish thanksgiving formula: "I thank you, Father, Lord of heaven and earth, because...". In his struggle at Gethsemane to accept his suffering and death, Jesus embodies the spirit of Old Testament lament psalms. According to Mark 15:34 and Matthew 27:46 Jesus died while reciting Psalm 22, which begins, "My God, my God, why have you forsaken me?" and ends with confident statements about the psalmist's vindication and even resurrection.

Two Versions of the Lord's Prayer

The Gospels of Matthew and Luke present slightly different forms of the Lord's Prayer. They may reflect the Greek versions used in Jewish Christian and gentile Christian communities, respectively. Both texts can be easily translated back into Aramaic, the language in which Jesus taught. The form and content of the Lord's Prayer undoubtedly reflect the voice of Jesus.

Because it is less familiar, Luke's version of the Lord's Prayer (11:2–4) may be the better place to begin. It consists of a simple address ("Father"), two "you" petitions regarding the coming kingdom ("[H]allowed be your name. Your kingdom come") and three "we" petitions about preparing for the coming kingdom—requests for physical sustenance ("our daily bread"), forgiveness of sins and protection in the trials and tribulations accompanying the kingdom's arrival.

Matthew's version (6:9–13) features a fuller address, beginning with a typical Jewish title for God: "Our Father in heaven." It contains an additional "you" petition: "Your will be done, on earth as it is in heaven." And it includes another "we" petition: "[R]escue us from the evil one." Adding to "fixed" prayer formulas was and is typical of Jewish prayer practice.

Praying for the Kingdom

The Lord's Prayer directly expresses the central themes of Jesus' preaching. He invites his followers to approach God as "Father" with the same spirit of intimacy and confidence that he himself displayed. The "you" petitions all express Jesus' hope for the full coming of God's kingdom and acknowledge that it is *God's* kingdom and *God's* task to bring it about among us and for us.

The first "we" petition recognizes our dependence on God for material and spiritual "bread" as we await and prepare for the coming kingdom. The second "we" petition declares that if we expect to obtain forgiveness from God at the Last Judgment and in the present, we must be willing to forgive those who have offended us. Matthew underlines the point by adding another saying to the prayer: "For if you forgive others their trespasses, your heavenly Father will also forgive you; but if you do not forgive others, neither will your Father forgive your trespasses" (6:14–15).

The third and final "we" petition warns that the full coming of God's kingdom will be accompanied by a period of severe testing, and that we should pray for divine protection and help. The traditional ending "For thine is the kingdom..." is not present in the oldest and most reliable manuscripts and is generally regarded as a later addition to "seal" or end the prayer. The Lord's Prayer soon became the equivalent of the Jewish Eighteen Benedictions, and was recited three times a day in some early Christian circles.

Ask, Search, Knock

Luke's Gospel presents two sections of Jesus' teachings about how to pray. Their surprising and challenging content bears the stamp of Jesus, the master teacher.

The parable of the friend at midnight encourages persistence and even shamelessness in bringing our petitions to God (11:5–8). It gives us permission to bother or pester God with our requests. Sayings about the power of prayer (11:9–10) may have become so familiar that we fail to grasp the magnitude of their claims: "Ask, and it will be given you; search, and you will find; knock, and the door will be opened for you. For everyone who asks receives, and everyone who searches finds, and for everyone who knocks, the door will be opened." They all express a remarkable confidence in God's willingness to answer prayers. There are no qualifications or nuances, and the "automatic" nature of the guarantees is surprising, even shocking.

The short parable that follows about the good gifts that a father wants to give ("If you then, who are evil, know how to give good gifts to your children, how much more will the heavenly Father give the Holy Spirit to those who ask him!" 11:13) is a further reminder that God wants very much to answer our prayers and to give us the Holy Spirit as the best gift of all.

Persist in Prayer

Two parables in Luke 18:1–14 emphasize persistence in prayer and humility before God. The parable of the widow and the unjust judge suggests that if an unjust judge will finally give in to the repeated requests of a widow—the most powerless and defenseless member of ancient Jewish society—will not God answer the requests of those who persist in prayer? Jesus assures us, "I tell you, he will quickly grant justice to them" (18:8).

In the second parable the Pharisee who goes up to the temple to pray represents the model of strict religious observance, while the tax collector can say only, "God, be merciful to me, a sinner" (18:13). Nevertheless, the humble prayer of the tax collector—who would have been suspected of dishonesty and disloyalty to the Jewish people—is heard by God, whereas the Pharisee's list of his own spiritual achievements is rejected as not being a prayer at all. Jesus' lesson here is "I tell you, this man [the tax collector] went down to his home justified rather than the other [the Pharisee]; for all who exalt themselves will be humbled, but all who humble themselves will be exalted" (18:14).

Jesus' Own Prayer

The prayer attributed to Jesus in John 17 expresses his sentiments as the Son of God. As he concludes the Last Supper and prepares for his passion and death, we hear Jesus speaking to his Father in a lengthy prayer that begins, "Father, the hour has come..." (17:1). He prays first for himself in order that his Father might glorify him as he, the Son, seeks to glorify the Father in his death and Resurrection. Then he prays for the disciples who are with him, that the Father may protect them, give them joy and make them holy. Finally, he prays for the church, that its members may be one and so share in the unity that exists between the Father and the Son. This prayer invites us believers into the life of the one God, who is Father, Son and Holy Spirit.

These Gospel texts about prayer undoubtedly reflect Jesus' own teaching on the subject. Using the language of Jewish prayer, Jesus teaches us to address God as a loving Father, to pray for the full coming of God's kingdom and to persist in our prayers of petition.

. . . .

W H E N   Y O U   P R A Y . . .

We know it by several names—the Lord's Prayer, the Our Father, the Paternoster (from the first two words of the Latin translation). We pray it at Mass, in the Liturgy of the Hours, as part of the rosary. Used by Catholic, Protestant and Orthodox Christians, it is perhaps the most ecumenical prayer in our tradition. However, Catholics generally omit the doxology ("For thine is the kingdom..."), which was added later.

At Mass the Lord's Prayer is introduced with these words: "Let us pray with confidence to the Father in the words our Savior gave us."[6] This prayer has been faithfully passed down from the time of Jesus. Matthew and Luke have slightly different versions of the prayer in their Gospels. The version that we use at Mass is closer to Matthew's, as his Gospel was long considered the best for teaching the faith. While some scholars believe that Jesus was simply offering a way to pray, rather than exact words, clearly his followers and most Christians after them have treasured these words as coming from the Lord himself.

The *Didache* (Greek for "teaching") is a document from the late first century that presents the "Teaching of the Twelve Apostles." It includes a version of the Lord's Prayer that is similar to Matthew's and the instruction to "pray this three times each day."

. . . .

QUESTIONS

• Jesus marked the most important moments of his life with prayer. What are the significant times in your life when you have turned to God in prayer?

• What is your favorite line or section of the Lord's Prayer? Does it challenge you? Bring you comfort? Express or offer you hope?

• Jesus was a person of prayer. Could people say the same about you? How can you make more time for prayer in your life?

CHAPTER SEVEN

· *Jesus and Women* ·

W as Jesus a feminist? Some might say it's not fair to pose this provocative question. One can easily object that feminism—the equality of women and men—is a late nineteenth-century western idea, and that it is unfair to impose it on a first-century Jew like Jesus.

The society in which Jesus lived and taught was patriarchal and hierarchical, that is, the husband was the head of the household, and women, children and slaves were subordinate to him. Roles and tasks were clearly divided between men and women.

Jesus and his first followers were people of their particular time and place. To act otherwise would have marked Jesus as a social deviant. Nevertheless, in comparison with other Jewish religious leaders of his day, Jesus was remarkably open to the participation of women in his movement. While descriptions of Jesus as a feminist or as promoting a discipleship of equals may exaggerate his openness, they do remind us of his boldness in giving place and prominence to women in his life and work.

The Mother of Jesus

In the Gospels Mary, the mother of Jesus, is most prominent at the beginning and end of Jesus' life. In Matthew's Gospel we learn that Mary was engaged to Joseph when "she was found to be with child from the Holy Spirit" (1:18). In the historical context of first-century Palestine, it is likely that Mary was young (thirteen or fourteen), that her marriage to Joseph had been arranged by older family members and that she was in the midst of a yearlong engagement period.

Luke presents Mary as one of the characters (along with Zechariah and Elizabeth, John the Baptist, the shepherds and Simeon and Anna) who represent the best in Israel's tradition. She willingly accepts her mission to become the mother of the Messiah.

After giving birth to Jesus, Mary observes the various rituals surrounding childbirth in the Jewish law and is warned in anticipation of Jesus' passion and death: "a sword will pierce your own soul too" (2:35). Years later she accompanies the twelve-year-old Jesus on a pilgrimage to Jerusalem at Passover.

In these various episodes Mary is described as one who accepts the word of God, believes that it was being fulfilled in her and reflects on what was said about her son. When the adult Jesus defines his true family as "those who hear the word of God and do it" (Luke 8:21), it is the mother of Jesus who emerges as the perfect example of discipleship.

Mary is the one person who remains with Jesus from birth to death. John's Gospel reveals that it was Mary's words to Jesus that occasioned his first miracle in turning water into wine. In John's passion narrative Mary appears at the foot of the cross along with the "beloved disciple." With the dying Jesus they form a community of compassion and provide a model for all Christian communities. According to the Acts of the Apostles, Mary was present with the twelve apostles and other disciples as they gathered in Jerusalem after the Ascension of Jesus and before the Holy Spirit came upon them at Pentecost.

Other Women in Jesus' Ministry

The women followers of Jesus are especially prominent in the Gospel accounts of his death and resurrection. They see Jesus die, they see where he was buried and they find his tomb empty on Easter Sunday.

In describing the women who witness Jesus' death and burial, Mark mentions in passing—almost as an afterthought—that several women had accompanied Jesus and his male disciples during his public ministry: They "used to follow him and provided for him when he was in Galilee; and there were many other women who had come up with him to Jerusalem" (15:41).

Luke, however, offers this surprising information much earlier in his account (8:1–3). He names three women—Mary Magdalene, Joanna the wife of Chuza, and Susanna—and adds that there were many other women who provided for Jesus and his male disciples. The question is sometimes asked: Who cooked the Last Supper? The most obvious answer is that these women did!

In the context of first-century Judaism, it would have been very surprising, if not scandalous, that a Jewish teacher and his male disciples would have been accompanied by women who were not their wives. Since this is not the kind of thing that early Christians would have invented, the presence of women in the Jesus movement seems well-founded on the historical level. But whether the male disciples regarded women as their equals is unlikely, given the patriarchal character of Jewish society at the time.

Mutual Faithfulness

In Jesus' public ministry women were frequently the recipients of his healing power. For example, he healed Peter's mother-in-law, the daughter of Jairus, the woman with the flow of blood and the daughter of the Syrophoenician woman. From his dialogue with the Syrophoenician woman, a non-Jew, he seems to have come to recognize more clearly that his mission was not to be limited to his fellow Jews. With his absolute prohibition of divorce, Jesus gave protection to women in a society in which a husband could divorce his wife merely by giving her a legal document and sending her out of his household (see Deuteronomy 24:1–4).

The Gospels agree that when Jesus was arrested, his male disciples fled but his women followers remained faithful, witnessed his death and burial and discovered his tomb empty. These facts were embarrassing to early Christians because they reflected badly on their male heroes. Moreover, since the testimony of women was not acceptable in Jewish courts of the time, the appeal to women as witnesses was not the kind of thing that Christians would have invented.

Mary Magdalene

The most prominent woman in the Gospel accounts of Jesus' death and resurrection is Mary of Magdala. (Magdala is a village on the western shore of the Sea of Galilee). She is generally named first in the lists of women witnesses and, according to Matthew and John, is the first to see the risen Jesus on Easter Sunday.

Luke's Gospel depicts Mary Magdalene as one of the Galilean women who accompanied Jesus throughout his public ministry. The description of her as one "from whom seven demons had gone out" (8:2) indicates that she had undergone an exorcism, presumably performed by Jesus.

Mary's reputation as a prostitute rests unfairly on the unwarranted identification of her with the sinful woman who enters a Pharisee's house and washes Jesus' feet with her tears, dries them with her hair and anoints them with expensive ointment (7:36–50). Mary Magdalene is introduced in Luke's Gospel shortly after this story; thus the confusion by many of Mary Magdalene with this unnamed sinful woman.

As she is portrayed in the New Testament, Mary Magdalene is best understood as a witness to the risen Jesus. She saw Jesus die, knew where he was buried, found his tomb empty and encountered him alive once more. The risen Jesus gives Mary the mission of telling the male disciples that he is truly alive again and is ascending to his Father. Thus it is customary to refer to Mary Magdalene as "the apostle to the apostles." In later writings such as the Gospel of Mary, a second- or third-century text, Mary Magdalene becomes the revealer of secret wisdom in the post-Resurrection age.

A Celibate Jew?

Despite the prominence of women in the ancient sources about Jesus, there is no evidence that Jesus had a wife. While this may have surprised his relatives and contemporaries, it appears that Jesus refrained from marriage primarily out of dedication to his mission of proclaiming God's kingdom.

The practice of celibacy (abstaining from sexual relations and marriage) was not common in ancient Judaism. Indeed, according to the *Babylonian Talmud*, Rabbi Eliezer said: "Any Jew who does not have a wife is not a man."[7] However, it appears that in Jesus' time, members of some Jewish religious groups (Therapeutae and Essenes) who lived a communal life similar to that of later Christian monks were celibate.

"For the Sake of the Kingdom"

There is no indication in any ancient Jewish or Christian source that either John the Baptist or Jesus was married or had children. The only explicit teaching about celibacy that is attributed to Jesus in the Gospels appears in Matthew 19:12: "For...there are eunuchs who have made themselves eunuchs for the sake of the kingdom of heaven." Jesus prefaces this teaching with a caution that this kind of celibacy is a gift from God and follows the teaching with a reminder that it is voluntary on the disciple's part.

Celibacy undertaken "for the sake of the kingdom" fits well with what we know to have been the focus of Jesus' life and preaching. In this context, Jesus' teaching about voluntary celibacy would be a sign of total dedication to God's kingdom similar to the parables about total commitment (treasure in a field, pearl of great value) in Matthew 13:44–46. There is no hint of contempt for the body or contempt for marriage and sexual activity.

Marriage Among the Followers of Jesus

Peter was certainly married, since we know that he had a mother-in-law (Mark 1:29–31). And Paul claims in his first letter to the Corinthians that Cephas, usually interpreted as another name for Peter, was accompanied by his wife on his apostolic journeys. We know nothing about the marital status of the rest of the apostles or other early followers of Jesus, although their itinerant lifestyle would hardly promote stable family life.

In his First Letter to the Corinthians, Paul promotes virginity, abstinence and celibacy as Christian ideals. Yet he does not appeal to the teaching or example of Jesus. For Paul celibacy was a help toward more fervent consecration to God and God's kingdom. Paul concludes that one "who refrains from marriage will do better" (7:38). He was careful, however, to insist that celibacy is a gift from God and not granted to everybody.

When Paul wrote his letters, he was not married and affirms that he was celibate. However, on the basis of 1 Corinthians 7:8 ("To the unmarried and the widows I say that it is well for them to remain unmarried as I am"), some interpreters argue that Paul had once been married and was then widowed.

The Role of Women in Jesus' Life and Ministry

Was Jesus a feminist? Not in the modern sense of the term. Jesus was a man of his own time and place. However, he was also ahead of his time culturally. He defined his true family as "those who hear the word of God and obey it" (Luke 11:28). Luke thought this was best expressed in Mary, the mother of Jesus.

Women played necessary and important roles in Jesus' public ministry and witnessed his death, burial and resurrection. The first appearance of the risen Jesus was to Mary Magdalene, who then served as the "apostle to the apostles." The voluntary celibacy embraced by Jesus and Paul is best understood not negatively, as a criticism of women or marriage, but rather positively, as flowing from their total commitment to God's kingdom.

. . . .

IMAGINING MARY MAGDALENE

In his book *Death of the Messiah*, Catholic Scripture scholar Raymond Brown wrote: "People who would never bother reading a responsible analysis of the traditions about how Jesus was crucified, died, was buried, and rose from the dead are fascinated by the report of some 'new insight' to the effect that he was not crucified or did not die, especially if the subsequent career involved running off with Mary Magdalene to India."[8]

Mary Magdalene fascinates a culture whose films, novels and gossip columns are dominated by romantic relationships. *The Da Vinci Code*, a recent fictional spin-off from the Gospels, portrays Mary Magdalene as the wife of Jesus, the mother of his child, Hebrew royalty and symbol of the sacred feminine— almost more significant than Jesus himself.

The Gospels are theological documents, not biographies or novels. But they remain our first and best source of information about Jesus and his followers. John's account of Mary Magdalene's tearful reunion with Jesus after the Resurrection might suggest a deeper personal relationship to our modern imaginations. But John is clear that Mary's role was always to proclaim the news of the risen Christ. Fictional accounts of Gospel figures can stir our imaginations, but in the end we need to seek the truth from more reliable sources.

.   .   .   .

QUESTIONS

• What stories of Jesus and women in the Gospels do you find most memorable? What message of challenge, comfort or hope do you hear in these stories?

• How well do you judge that our church has followed Jesus' lead in regard to inclusion of and respect for the gifts of women? How is your own parish doing in this regard?

• What woman in your life has been most influential in helping you along your faith journey? Find a way to express your appreciation to her.

CHAPTER EIGHT

· *Jesus and Politics* ·

In recent United States political campaigns, religion and politics have played a major role. Some candidates have tried to outdo their rivals in professing religious piety, while others have promised to do everything possible to maintain the historic wall of separation between church and state. Behind these debates we hear the echoes of Jesus' words of caution about rendering to Caesar what belongs to Caesar and rendering to God what belongs to God (Mark 12:17).

In Jesus' time religion, politics and economics were mixed together, much more so than they are in modern western democracies. Jesus was a preacher of God's kingdom and a teacher of wisdom rather than a political scientist, a politician or an economist. Nevertheless, his teachings had political and economic implications that got him into trouble with the Jewish political and religious leaders as well as the Roman imperial officials. His teachings about the kingdom of God and justice were surely factors in his arrest, condemnation and execution.

Jewish Background

Throughout Israel's long history, its people lived under many different political systems. The Hebrew people first took shape as slaves in Egypt under the all-powerful Pharaoh and found freedom under Moses' leadership by fleeing from Pharaoh's army. On entering the Promised Land of Canaan around 1200 BC, the Israelites developed a loose confederacy. It was bound together by a covenant and dependent upon judges, charismatic leaders who arose in times of crisis and rescued their people.

Recognizing the need for greater unity and stability, Israel, around 1000 BC, opted for the model of kingship, which was common in surrounding nations. All authority was in the hands of powerful kings like David and Solomon. After a promising start, the monarchy soon divided into a northern kingdom (Israel) and a southern kingdom (Judah). Neither kingdom produced many good leaders. Israel fell to the Assyrians in the late eighth century BC, and Judah fell to the Babylonians in the early sixth century BC.

With the end of the monarchy in 587 BC, the Judeans (from the southern kingdom) experienced life under various foreign empires: Babylonian, Persian, Greek and Roman. Some of these, like the Persians, were less intrusive than others and were satisfied as long as the peace was maintained and taxes were paid. Others, like the Seleucid Greeks under Antiochus IV Epiphanes (175–164 BC), were eager to integrate the Jews fully into their empire even in matters of religion and culture.

In their efforts to defend themselves against the Seleucids, Jewish leaders known as the Maccabees appealed to Rome to become their ally and protector in the mid-second century. By the time of Jesus, Judea was under the direct political control of a Roman governor, or prefect, named Pontius Pilate. Galilee in the north was ruled by Herod Antipas, one of the sons of Herod the Great and a political tool of the Romans. The Romans were primarily concerned with exploiting the resources of their subject peoples, keeping the peace and collecting taxes from them. Their policy was to react swiftly and brutally to any threat to their power. Most Jews were able and willing to deal with different political systems as long as their rights to worship the God of Israel and observe their ancestral laws were respected. What they could not accept was any attempt to replace their God with another god or with the emperor or being forced to act against their religious traditions.

Politics

There were varying degrees of dissatisfaction with Roman imperial rule in the Jewish society of Jesus' day. The hope was strong that God would soon intervene to liberate his people and fulfill his promises to them. In this context, Jesus' teachings about the coming kingdom could sound revolutionary and politically dangerous. But there is no firm evidence that he was in sympathy with the violent Jewish revolutionary group known as the Zealots.

Jesus was a popular teacher who drew crowds of Jews, many of whom were looking forward to the coming kingdom. Even though the thrust of Jesus' teaching was against violence, his popularity among members of a subject people made him suspect to the Roman officials and to some Jewish leaders who wished to preserve the status quo. To them, the religious movement that centered on Jesus looked like a political—perhaps even a military—movement. To them, Jesus' message that God alone is king and that his kingdom will soon be made manifest sounded like a call for revolution.

In the Gospels the closest Jesus comes to commenting on the Roman Empire is the famous "render to Caesar" passages in Mark 12:13–17 (see also Matthew 22:15–22; Luke 20:20–26). This text springs from a series of debates or controversies between Jesus and

various groups of opponents in Jerusalem. His questioners are identified as Pharisees and Herodians. The Pharisees, a Jewish religious
fraternity, had a long history of involvement in Jewish politics, and
here their role is most likely to represent religious Jews opposed to
the Romans. The Herodians supported the Herod family and were
therefore aligned with the Romans.

The question both groups put to Jesus is: "Is it lawful to pay
taxes to the emperor, or not?" (Mark 12:14). The query was intended
to trap Jesus. If he said "no," then he was in trouble with the
Herodians and the Romans. If he said "yes," he would lose the sup-
port of the local Jewish population—especially the religiously
observant—who wanted the Romans to leave and to have their own
people in charge.

Sensing a trap and recognizing its possible consequences, Jesus
gives an indirect answer by responding with another question. He
asks for a coin and inquires about whose image and inscription are
on it. (They would have been those of the emperor Tiberius who
ruled from AD 14 to 37.) The entire story is really an introduction
leading to Jesus' pronouncement: "Give to the emperor the things
that are the emperor's, and to God the things that are God's" (12:17).

Since Jews in Palestine were using the emperor's coins and par-
ticipating in his political and economic system, they had already
taken upon themselves the duty of paying taxes to the emperor. Thus
the Herodians could have no objection to Jesus' answer. By challenging his questioners to be as diligent in observing their obligations to
God as they were to the emperor and his officials, Jesus diffused any
complaints the religiously observant Pharisees could have had. All
the while, Jesus remained true to his own principles that God is the
real king over all creation and deserves more respect and service
than any earthly ruler does.

This passage illustrates Jesus' cautious acceptance of Roman
rule. Some early Christians, like Paul (in Romans 13:1–7), were eager
to show that they could be good citizens of the Roman Empire at its

best. Others, like John (in Revelation), urged nonviolent resistance to local efforts at forcing Christians to worship the emperor and the goddess Roma, the personification of the empire. The crucial issue was always the extent to which the ruler was to be regarded as divine; the risk was that the imperial officials might force Christians to acknowledge him as superior to "our Lord Jesus Christ."

Economics

As an observant Jew, Jesus stood in the great biblical tradition of social justice and social concern for the poor. He took over and adapted many of the Old Testament's teachings on these matters, and in some cases he challenged his followers to go beyond them. While not an economist or a social planner, Jesus offered wise and provocative teachings that had economic and social implications for those who took them seriously.

There are several different attitudes toward poverty and the poor in the Old Testament. On the one hand, God is regarded as the protector of the poor, the poor depend on God, people ought to be kind to the poor, and in the age to come the roles of rich and poor will be reversed. On the other hand, the wealthy oppress the poor and cause poverty. Poverty is thought by some to be the result of foolish decisions that people make, and the presence of the poor is seen as a sign of Israel's unfaithfulness to its covenant with God. Of course in some circumstances all of these statements are true, and no single one exhausts the topic.

While the right to possess property is assumed in the Old Testament, it is also assumed that God is the ultimate owner of the land and that the people are hereditary tenants on God's property. Many elements of the biblical laws were intended to protect poor people: creating provisions for freeing slaves, observing sabbatical and jubilee years when debts were forgiven, leaving crops in the field at harvest time for the poor to take, challenging the rich to share their goods with the poor and criticizing greed and avarice.

There are three major strands in Jesus' teachings about wealth and poverty. According to the first strand, poverty can be a positive personal good. This attitude is expressed in the beatitude: "Blessed are you who are poor, for yours is the kingdom of God" (Luke 6:20). The "poor" are in a position of unique openness to God because they have correctly recognized that we humans are totally dependent on God. Those whose life is focused on the service of God without concern for earthly goods will share in the fullness of God's kingdom.

The second strand appears mainly in Jesus' instructions to his disciples as he sends them out on their missions: "Take nothing for your journey, no staff, nor bag, nor bread, nor money—not even an extra tunic" (Luke 9:3; see also Matthew 10:5–15; Mark 6:6–13). Jesus insists on simplicity of lifestyle from his followers—not for its own sake but in the context of their mission of proclaiming God's kingdom and bringing healing to those in need.

There is also here a strong conviction that riches and possessions are obstacles to serving and attaining God's kingdom. This attitude is clearly expressed in Jesus' saying about not trying to serve two masters: "You cannot serve God and wealth" (Matthew 6:24). Contrary to the assumptions of many of his Jewish contemporaries, including his apostles, Jesus contends that it is very hard for rich people to enter the kingdom of heaven. When a man comes to him seeking to know how to inherit eternal life, Jesus advises him to "go, sell what you own, and give the money to the poor, and you will have treasure in heaven; then come, follow me." Then, speaking to his disciples, Jesus says, "How hard it will be for those who have wealth to enter the kingdom of God!" (Mark 10:21, 23).

The third strand emphasizes the need for the rich to share their material possessions with the poor in this world. This teaching is most memorably illustrated by Jesus' parable of the rich man and Lazarus in Luke 16:19–31. Lazarus, the poor beggar, lies outside the gate of the rich man's house, while inside the rich man is splendidly dressed and enjoys the best of food and drink in total ignorance of Lazarus' existence. When both men die, their positions are reversed, with the rich man being in Hades (hell) and the poor man in Abraham's bosom (heaven). Then it is too late for the rich man to share his material possessions and to rest in Abraham's bosom as a reward for doing so. The point of the parable is that the appropriate time to share one's goods with the poor and to combat the evils of economic poverty is now—before it is too late.

RELIGION AND POLITICS: A VOLATILE MIX

The spiritual or religious impulse, for most people, is deeply rooted in the core of their being. Our relationship with God is intertwined with our creation, continued existence, death and afterlife. This makes religion a powerful emotional compass, directing people to unimaginable heroic efforts on behalf of humanity—or equally unimaginable acts of destruction. When religion or religious rhetoric mix with nationalism, whether it's a group in power or a group being oppressed, the outcome is nearly always volatile.

We see this mix at the time of Jesus, in the Zealot movement and other groups seeking to throw off Roman oppression. We see it throughout the Old Testament, as the chosen people battle for control of the Promised Land. And tragically we see it in our own day in nearly every part of the world. The ongoing Israeli-Palestinian conflict, the terrorist organizations that have arisen from Islamic fundamentalism and the "God is on our side" rhetoric of fundamentalist Christians are but three prominent examples.

Jesus told his followers, "My kingdom is not from this world." He steadfastly refused to be exploited by the political movements of his day. Along with the Hebrews he insists that ours is a God of all people and all nations. Only the full gospel message of peace can uncover the dangers inherent in mixing sectarian religious beliefs and nationalism.

. . . .

QUESTIONS

- How much do your faith and religious convictions enter into your political and economic choices? How much do you think they should?

- What do you believe Jesus' position would be on some of the controversial political issues facing your government today? Are your judgments based on your values, gospel values or both?

- How do Jesus' teachings about wealth and poverty challenge your attitudes about the poor? Your material concerns and choices? Your actions on behalf of the poor? Choose one attitude or behavior that you will work on this week to make it better reflect that of Christ's.

CHAPTER NINE

· *The Death of Jesus* ·

Whenen we Christians make our profession of faith with the
Apostles' Creed every Sunday, we say: "For our sake he [Jesus] was
crucified under Pontius Pilate; he suffered, died and was buried."
This statement, so familiar to us, raises three questions that are piv-
otal in our historical portrait of Jesus: What circumstances led to
Jesus' death? Who killed Jesus? Why did Jesus die?

Sources

The accounts of Jesus' passion and death in the four Gospels agree
on many basic points. They tell us that Jesus was arrested, underwent two hearings or trials, was sentenced to death by crucifixion
and died on a cross. Mark's passion narrative seems to have been the
earliest; indeed, large blocks of it may have existed even before he
completed his Gospel around AD 70. Matthew and Luke both used
Mark as a source and included material from other traditions as

well. John's Gospel represents a separate tradition, while agreeing with Mark on many points.

None of the four Evangelists set out to write a detailed chronicle of the day on which Jesus died, though all of them provide some reliable historical details. Their real interest lay in the theological significance of Jesus' death for us and for our sins, and how his death took place according to the Old Testament.

Roman Responsibility

The best clue toward determining who killed Jesus is found in the way he died—by crucifixion. In Jesus' time, crucifixion was a Roman punishment inflicted mainly on slaves and revolutionaries. The usual Jewish mode of execution was stoning, as in the case of Stephen (Acts 7:54–60). Crucifixion was a cruel and public way to die. It was meant to shame the one being executed and to deter onlookers from doing what he had done.

The official who had the power to execute Jesus by crucifixion was the Roman governor or prefect of Judea, Pontius Pilate. Jesus was put to death "under Pontius Pilate" around the year 30 AD. Although the Gospels present Pilate as indecisive and somewhat concerned for justice in Jesus' case, the Alexandrian Jewish writer Philo, a contemporary of Jesus, described Pilate as "inflexible, merciless and obstinate."[9]

All four Gospels recount a proceeding or hearing in which Jesus appeared before Pontius Pilate. In the Gospels of Matthew, Mark and Luke, Pilate questions Jesus and offers the crowd a choice between Barabbas (a convicted criminal) and Jesus. At the urging of the chief priests, the crowd calls for Barabbas to be released and for Jesus to be crucified. Pilate bows to their pressure and has Jesus scourged and handed over to be put to death. John's elaborate account of Jesus' trial before Pilate also ends with Pilate handing over Jesus to be executed.

The official charge leveled against Jesus appears in the inscription placed on the cross: "the King of the Jews." To Christians, this title ironically expresses the truth that Jesus really was the Messiah of Jewish expectations. To Pilate and the Jewish leaders, however, Jesus was one in a series of Jewish religious-political troublemakers intent on destroying the Roman Empire and the status quo at Jerusalem in the name of the kingdom of God. Josephus described some of these Jewish messiah figures in his *Jewish Antiquities*. They often used religious symbols and traditions to gain a popular following and to begin an uprising. The Roman officials dealt with them swiftly and brutally.

Jesus did not die alone. Rather, he was crucified along with two men described in various translations as "thieves," "bandits," "rebels" or "revolutionaries"—the same Greek word Mark applied to Barabbas (15:7). While the Evangelists were quick to deny that Jesus was one of them, it is likely that Pilate viewed him as another one of those Jewish religious-political rebels.

So the manner of Jesus' death (crucifixion), the legal system in force (with Pilate having ultimate authority in capital cases), the official charge against Jesus ("the King of the Jews") and the type of persons crucified along with him (thieves, bandits, rebels, revolutionaries) all point to the conclusion that the ultimate legal and moral responsibility for Jesus' death lay with the Roman prefect, Pontius Pilate.

The Role of the Jews
How Pilate came to be prefect of Judea is important in assessing Jewish responsibility for Jesus' death. With the success of the Maccabean revolt in the mid-second century BC, Judea gained political independence as well as a powerful protector in Rome. The Romans were called upon not only to defend the Maccabean dynasty from its foreign enemies but also to resolve internal and even family disputes.

Herod the Great married into the Maccabean priestly ruling family and served as a king in the service of the Romans from 40 to 4 BC. Upon Herod's death, the region of Judea was assigned to one of his sons, Herod Archelaus. After ten years of turmoil and rebellion, the Romans decided to take direct control of Judea by appointing a Roman prefect or governor in AD 6. The most famous of these was Pontius Pilate, who governed Judea from AD 26 to 36.

It was Roman policy to work with local peoples. When things got out of hand, the Roman armies would intervene with brutal force. In normal times, however, the Romans relied on local officials to collect taxes and keep the peace. So in Judea it was natural that there would be Jews who were willing to do the Romans' bidding.

Jerusalem was a pilgrimage center for Jews living in Judea and beyond. Three times a year—at the feasts of Passover, Weeks and Tabernacles—Jews came in large numbers to worship at the temple. The pilgrimage trade was a major industry in Jerusalem. The restoration and expansion of the temple, begun as part of Herod the Great's ambitious building program, was likewise a major industry. To a great extent, the chief priests and elders in Jerusalem oversaw this project.

The pilgrimages brought many people to Jerusalem. The themes of the great festivals, especially Passover with its commemoration of ancient Israel's liberation from slavery in Egypt, could easily incite nationalistic fervor and rebellion. So it was customary that the Roman prefect, whose official residence was in Caesarea Maritima on the Mediterranean seacoast, would come to Jerusalem to work with the local Jewish leaders to keep matters under control. They all had the same goal—to keep the peace.

Each Gospel recounts Jesus appearing at a trial or hearing before the Jewish council presided over by the high priest. The Jews who took the initiative in this proceeding were not the Pharisees (opponents of Jesus during his public ministry) but those who had the most stake in the smooth running of the temple and the peace of Jerusalem: the chief priests and elders.

According to Mark, there were two charges made against Jesus: He threatened to destroy the temple and in three days, to "build another, not made with hands" (14:58), and he claimed to be "the Messiah, the Son of the Blessed One" (14:61). There was surely some historical basis for these allegations.

Jesus' threat against the temple fits with his symbolic prophetic action in "cleansing" the temple (Mark 11:15–19) and his prophecy about its destruction (Mark 13:1–2). For the Jewish leaders, merchants and construction workers whose livelihood depended on the smooth running of the temple, the slightest threat against the temple—even a symbolic one—would have been taken very seriously.

Talk about Jesus as "the Messiah, the Son of the Blessed One" surely would have set off alarms, not only among the Romans but also among the Jewish leaders. Both viewed Jesus as another religious-political messianic pretender who had to be dealt with quickly. The kind of language being used about Jesus in some circles alerted them to the danger that he might pose to their power and to the status quo.

The Gospels suggest that the Jewish leaders were the prime movers in getting Jesus executed and that the Romans only ratified their decision. At the other end of the spectrum, however, some scholars argue that no Jewish authority was involved in any way. Between these two extremes there are mediating positions. Some scholars say that the Romans were the prime movers and that the Jewish authorities reluctantly gave in to pressure from them. Others state that, even though Jewish leaders were actively involved, the Romans carried out the main legal formalities.

Two important points emerge: Jesus was executed "under Pontius Pilate" and the Jewish authorities at Jerusalem very likely played some role in getting Jesus killed. Whatever Jewish

JESUS : A HISTORICAL PORTRAIT

responsibility there may have been lay with a small group (the chief priests and elders) in a specific place (Jerusalem) and at a specific time (Passover of AD 30). The people's response in Matthew 27:25, "His blood be on us and on our children!" is best taken as referring to the crowd ("us") manipulated by their leaders and to the destruction of Jerusalem in AD 70 ("our children"), not to the whole Jewish people for all ages.

The official position of the Catholic church is clearly stated in Vatican II's Declaration on the Relation of the Church to Non-Christian Religions *(Nostra Aetate)*: "Even though the Jewish authorities and those who followed their lead pressed for the death of Christ (cf. John 19:6), neither all Jews indiscriminately at that time, nor Jews today, can be charged with the crimes committed during his passion."[10]

Christians today need to be sensitive to the tendency in the Gospels to emphasize the responsibility of the Jewish leaders in Jesus' death and to play down the role of the Romans. One can get the impression that the Jewish leaders simply manipulated Pilate to pass sentence on Jesus, and that he turned Jesus over to them to be executed.

The impression grows as one moves from Mark to Matthew and Luke, who used Mark as their main source. Moreover, John's Gospel lumps all of Jesus' opponents under the title "the Jews," thus apparently extending Jewish responsibility beyond the chief priests and elders. Of course, Jesus and his first followers were all Jews.

Such passages need to be read in their late first-century historical context: Jerusalem had been destroyed and Christians were accommodating themselves to life within the Roman Empire. When removed from that historical context, these texts can contribute to anti-Semitism and obscure the Jewishness of Jesus as well as the Jewish character of early Christianity.

Three Questions

We began by raising three pivotal questions about the death of Jesus. Now we can better answer them. (1) What circumstances led to Jesus' death? On the historical level, one can point to the sinful social structures in first-century Palestine and the spiral of violence that led Pilate to view Jesus as a dangerous Jewish rebel. On the theological level one can say that Jesus' death on the cross was the result of our human sinfulness. (2) Who killed Jesus? Pontius Pilate, with cooperation from some Jewish leaders in Jerusalem, killed Jesus. (3) Why did Jesus die? The New Testament writers give several profound theological responses: Jesus died in accord with God's will as expressed in the Scriptures (Matthew). Jesus died a sacrificial death for us and for our sins (Mark, Paul, Hebrews). In his death Jesus gave us an example of fidelity in suffering (Luke). Jesus' death was part of his work in revealing God and of his glorious return to the Father (John), as well as the pledge of his Second Coming (Revelation).

WHO KILLED JESUS?

Mel Gibson's 2005 film *The Passion of the Christ* raised a familiar controversy over the portrayal of the role of the Jews in the death of Jesus.

For centuries persecution of Jews was given an emotional boost by yearly passion plays. In the Middle Ages peasants with little education received much of their knowledge of Bible stories from morality plays, dramatizations of the great events in salvation history. Without our own access to modern scholarship and nuanced treatments of Scripture, they made an erroneous connection between the Jewish people living in medieval Europe and the small group of Jewish leaders in Jerusalem at the time of Jesus. Critics of *The Passion of the Christ* argued that many of the portrayals in the film shared some of the stereotypes often used in the past two thousand years to implicate Jews in Jesus' death. The Vatican and the bishops in the United States have declared that any dramatic portrayals of Jesus' passion and death must not implicate all Jews of any time or place: "...any presentations that explicitly or implicitly seek to shift responsibility from human sin onto this or that historical group, such as the Jews, can only be said to obscure a core gospel truth."[11]

. . . .

QUESTIONS

• When you look at a crucifix, do you consider the emotional and physical agony of Jesus' death? Why do you think Jesus had to die in such a humiliating and painful way?

• There is still a great deal of lingering anti-Semitism, much of it related to the Jews' perceived role in Jesus' death. How does the above explanation of their role help you? Does it change any of your own prejudices?

• How does Jesus' death make a difference in your life? Take some time this week to share your response with him in prayer.

CHAPTER TEN

• *The Resurrection of Jesus* •

The boldest claim that early Christians made was that their teacher and hero, Jesus of Nazareth, who died and was buried, was raised from the dead.

This claim was so extraordinary that those who heard Peter preaching at Pentecost assumed that he and the other disciples had been drinking too much new wine (Acts 2:13). When Paul preached to a Greek audience in Athens, they were receptive to his message until he said that God confirmed Jesus' message by raising him from the dead. The Acts of the Apostles tells us, "When they heard of the resurrection...some began to scoff" (17:32).

Resurrection means the restoration of a person to bodily life after death. It is not the same as the immortality of the soul, since resurrection involves the whole person, body and soul, in a restoration to life. Neither is it the same as resuscitation, since the resuscitated person will eventually die again and not be brought back to life.

The first followers of Jesus believed that Jesus, having died on the cross and having been buried in a tomb owned by Joseph of Arimathea, was miraculously restored to life by the one whom he called his "Father." What did early Christians believe about the resurrection of Jesus? Why did they believe this?

Jewish Background

The early parts of the Old Testament bear witness to some belief in life after death. The ancient Israelites imagined that the dead went to Sheol (the abode of the dead) and lived on in some shadowy kind of existence. Sheol was neither heaven nor hell. Rather, it was something in between, a dark and gloomy place (the "pit"), whose inhabitants could neither find much happiness nor praise God (see Psalm 88).

In the sixth century BC some of the prophets began to describe their hope for Israel's future in terms of resurrection. For example, we find in Isaiah 26:19 the statement: "Your dead shall live, their corpses shall rise." In his vision of the valley of the dry bones, Ezekiel portrays the revival of Israel in exile as a collective resurrection of the dead: "[T]he breath came into them, and they lived" (37:10). In both cases, however, resurrection serves as a metaphor for the rebirth of God's people, not as a description of what happens to individuals after death.

The book of Daniel, written in the second century BC, provides the first explicit description of the resurrection of dead persons: "Many of those who sleep in the dust of the earth shall awake, some to everlasting life, and some to shame and everlasting contempt" (12:2). Belief in the resurrection of persons appears also in the book of Wisdom: "[T]he souls of the righteous are in the hand of God" (3:1). In the martyrdom of the mother and her seven sons in 2 Maccabees 7, one son, at his last breath, proclaims that "the King of the universe will raise us up to an everlasting renewal of life, because we have died for his laws" (2 Maccabees 7:9).

Those Jews in Jesus' time who believed in the resurrection of the dead expected that it would take place at the end of history (as part of the full coming of God's kingdom), that it would involve most everyone (the general judgment) and that the just or righteous would enjoy eternal life with God as whole persons, body and soul.

Among the various Jewish groups, the Pharisees were the great proponents of resurrection, while the Sadducees rejected it as not present in the Old Testament Law. In this matter Jesus sided with the Pharisees. According to Mark (12:18–27) Jesus argued against the Sadducees, holding that reference to the resurrection can be found in the book of Exodus and that resurrected life is not exactly the same as earthly life.

Against this background we can see how extraordinary belief in the resurrection of Jesus was—and is. The early Christians claimed that Jesus, as an individual, had been restored to life after his death before the end of history, that many who knew him before he died experienced him as once again fully alive, and that his resurrection provides the basis of hope for the resurrection of us all and for eternal life in God's kingdom.

The Empty Tomb

Jesus died on a Friday, most likely in early April of AD 30. According to John he died about the time when the Passover lambs were being sacrificed in the Jerusalem temple complex. Jesus' burial was arranged by Joseph of Arimathea, who offered to have the corpse interred in a new tomb that he owned. Jerusalem in Jesus' time has been described as a city surrounded by a huge cemetery. The tombs were not holes dug in the ground but rather caves cut out of the soft limestone all around the city.

The Jewish Sabbath begins at sundown on Friday, so whatever work was needed to transport Jesus' body and prepare it for burial had to be done immediately after his death. All the Evangelists report that Mary Magdalene and other women followers witnessed Jesus' death and burial.

When Jesus' body arrived at the burial cave, it would have been treated with perfumes and spices (to control the odor) and laid out on a platform cut into the rock. There it would have been left for a year or so, allowing the flesh to disintegrate. All this time, a large stone, probably in the shape of a large tire or doughnut, would have blocked the tomb's entrance to discourage robbers. At the end of the year, the bones would be gathered and placed in a stone box called an *ossuary* ("bone box"), which might be inscribed with the name of the deceased. At least this would have been the plan.

All the Gospels agree that Mary Magdalene and other women came to Jesus' tomb on Easter Sunday morning and found it empty. They had seen where Jesus was buried, so they did not lose their way and go to the wrong tomb. They went there to complete the preparation of Jesus' body, because the onset of the Sabbath had forced them to leave before they had finished.

They wondered how they might enter the cave, given the large stone placed at the mouth of the tomb. But when the women arrived, they found that the stone had already been moved and the tomb was empty. They were informed by a "young man" or an angel: "Do not be alarmed; you are looking for Jesus of Nazareth, who was crucified. He has been raised; he is not here" (Mark 16:6).

How is it that the tomb came to be empty? The Jewish opponents of Jesus spread the rumor that Jesus' disciples had stolen his body. Others argued that the women went to the wrong tomb, even though the Gospels name them as witnesses to the burial of Jesus. Still others suggest that Jesus awoke from a coma and somehow got out of the cave. However, the only ancient sources that we have—the Gospels—all agree that the tomb was empty because Jesus had been raised from the dead.

The Appearances
The fact that Jesus' tomb was found to be empty does not in itself prove his resurrection. But it is a necessary precondition for belief in

his resurrection. More convincing are the many accounts of early Christians who testified that they experienced Jesus as alive in a bodily way after his death.

In a very early summary of Christian faith (1 Corinthians 15:3–8), Paul provides a list of persons to whom the risen Jesus appeared: Cephas (another name for Peter), the twelve apostles, a crowd of five hundred, James, all the apostles and Paul himself. When Paul wrote his letter (around AD 55), most of these persons were still alive and presumably could be questioned about their experiences.

Paul's list of those to whom the risen Jesus appeared grows when we take account of the appearance narratives at the end of each Gospel. In Matthew's Gospel the risen Jesus appeared to the women who came to the tomb and the eleven disciples in Galilee. In Luke he appeared to two disciples on the road to Emmaus and to his disciples in Jerusalem. In John he appeared to Mary Magdalene and to his disciples without and with Thomas. Then he appeared in Galilee to seven disciples, including Peter and the beloved disciple. Mark's account (16:9–20) is generally regarded as a second-century summary of the appearances in other Gospels.

The various appearance stories differ in many details. What they have in common is that the recipients knew Jesus before his death and knew that he had died. These persons, not without difficulty, came to recognize the figure that they encountered as the risen Jesus. This risen Jesus is both pure spirit (he passes through walls) and yet still physical (he shares meals). In Luke's story of the journey to Emmaus, Jesus interprets the Old Testament Scriptures and eats with his disciples, actions that suggest connections with the Eucharist. Many of the post-resurrection stories feature the theme of mission in which Jesus sends forth his disciples to proclaim the Good News.

These stories have been interpreted by skeptics as visions, dreams or wish fulfillments. But that so many different persons could have been deceived seems unlikely. Early Christians interpreted these experiences as proof that Jesus had been raised from the dead.

The Early Christian Movement

Perhaps the strongest proof of the resurrection of Jesus is the survival and continuation of the movement he had begun. The entire New Testament affirms that the first followers of Jesus underwent a remarkable transformation after his death.

Three well-established historical facts pertaining to Jesus' last days were that (1) Judas, one of his closest followers, betrayed him at the time of his arrest, (2) at the same time his male followers abandoned him out of fear and (3) Peter denied even knowing Jesus. After the resurrection, however, those who had abandoned Jesus and fled out of fear proclaimed the gospel fearlessly.

What happened to bring about such a dramatic change? It must have been their experiences of Jesus as raised from the dead and restored to life in addition to the Pentecost.

The development in language and theology about Jesus in the twenty years between his death and the composition of the earliest complete document contained in the New Testament (1 Thessalonians) has been described as an "explosion" (see the next chapter). In the very first line of his letter, Paul, a monotheistic Jew, refers to Jesus as "the Lord Jesus Christ" and places him on the same level as "God the Father."

The historical evidence for the resurrection of Jesus consists of three strands: the empty tomb, the appearances of the risen Jesus and the success of the early Christian movement. No one of them alone definitively proves that Jesus rose from the dead. But taken together, they indicate that the best explanation is that Jesus "was raised on the third day in accordance with the scriptures" (1 Corinthians 15:4).

DANIEL J. HARRINGTON, S.J.

"RESURRECTION OF THE BODY AND LIFE EVERLASTING"

Jesus' resurrection was more than a miracle in itself. It represents a promise to his followers that they, too, will be raised up. Therefore, in the Apostles' Creed we profess our belief in "the resurrection of the body"—not just Jesus' body, but ours as well.

This belief was articulated as early as Paul's First Letter to the Corinthians: "But in fact Christ has been raised from the dead, the first fruits of those who have died.... [A]ll will be made alive in Christ" (1 Corinthians 15:20, 22).

Death becomes our entry into the fullness of the Christian life we accepted at our baptisms. Paul wrote to the Romans: "[W]e have been buried with him by baptism into death, so that, as Christ was raised from the dead by the glory of the Father, so we too might walk in newness of life.... [I]f we have been united with him in a death like his, we will certainly be united with him in a resurrection like his" (6:4–8). In the Catholic funeral liturgy, the casket is covered with a white pall that represents the person's baptismal garment. The prayers reflect a firm belief in the resurrection. The preface to the Eucharistic Prayer declares, "Lord, for your faithful people, life is changed, not ended."[12]

QUESTIONS

- What difference does it make in your life that Christ is risen? Imagine your life without this belief. How would you be different, live differently? In what would you put your hope?

- How compelling are the arguments explaining the empty tomb made by Jewish opponents of Jesus? Why do you believe in Christ's resurrection?

- Many of Jesus' post-resurrection appearances included the theme of mission, with Jesus sending forth the disciples to proclaim the Good News. How are you living out your mission as one saved by Jesus' death and resurrection?

CHAPTER ELEVEN

· *Jesus and the First Christians* ·

W e often hear historians speak about the *development* of the early Christian church, which conveys a sense of gradual progress spread over a relatively long period of time. A word that better describes the quick rise of the Christian movement is *explosion.*

The speed with which the early Christians developed a rich and sophisticated vocabulary and theology is historically amazing. Within the twenty years between Jesus' death and the first letter we have from Paul (1 Thessalonians), these followers produced many professions of faith, hymns, titles for Jesus and distinctive rituals. The marvelous creativity of the early Christians provides a powerful witness to the person of Jesus, his resurrection and the work of the Holy Spirit.

This chapter will look at how the first Christians understood and celebrated the risen Jesus, and why and how they believed that he was alive and guiding their movement even as he lived in glory with his Father.

Faith Statements

The earliest complete documents in the New Testament are the letters of Paul. All (except for Romans) were written between AD 51 and 58 to various Christian communities that he had founded. In his missionary work Paul focused on the significance of Jesus' death and resurrection for the lives of those who had entered into Christian faith. He sought always to connect the paschal mystery with the problems and opportunities of those whom he loved and directed.

At several points in his letters, Paul quoted what most scholars have agreed were already formulated statements of early Christian belief about Jesus. These statements originated sometime between Jesus' death and the composition of Paul's letters. The ways that Paul used them suggest that they were regarded as common beliefs about Jesus that were held by most early Christians, or at least those to whom he was writing.

In 1 Corinthians, Paul affirms "that Christ died for our sins in accordance with the scriptures, and that he was buried, and that he was raised on the third day in accordance with the scriptures, and that he appeared to Cephas [Peter], then to the twelve" (15:3–5). This faith statement takes Jesus' death and resurrection as one great event, interprets it as taking place according to God's will as expressed in the Old Testament and describes its saving significance for us all.

At the beginning of his Letter to the Romans, Paul sets out to establish common ground with Christians he has not yet met personally. So he used an existing faith statement to define what he means by the "gospel." This statement (1:3–4) asserts that the resurrection was the moment of Jesus' victory over death and his full revelation as the Son of God.

The idea of Christ's death as an effective sacrifice for sins also appears in another faith statement in Romans when Paul speaks of "Christ Jesus, whom God put forward as a sacrifice of atonement by his blood" (3:25).

In Galatians, Paul cites what was very likely a profession of faith associated with baptism: "There is no longer Jew or Greek, there is no longer slave or free, there is no longer male and female; for all of you are one in Christ Jesus" (3:28). Neither Paul nor the early Christians imagined that all ethnic, social or gender distinctions had instantly disappeared with baptism. But they were convinced that these differences were not nearly as important as their new identity as members of God's people in Christ.

Hymns

There is also good reason to believe that Paul's letters and other New Testament writings contain fragments of early Christian hymns. Pliny the Younger, one of the pagan observers of the early Christians, noted that they sang "a hymn to Christ as to a god"[13] in their Sunday gatherings.

One such hymn appears in Paul's Letter to the Philippians 2:6–11. Though it is not a hymn we recognize today, it celebrates key themes: the incarnation, death, resurrection and ascension of Jesus. It evokes the Old Testament figure of the Suffering Servant described in Isaiah 53: "he emptied himself, taking the form of a slave," insists that Jesus willingly went to his death in obedience to his heavenly Father, and celebrates his resurrection as an exaltation so that all creation should respond that "Jesus Christ is Lord" (2:11).

Other hymns celebrated Jesus as the Wisdom of God, much as some Old Testament texts (Proverbs 8; Sirach 24; Wisdom 7) poetically portray Wisdom as a female figure reflecting the presence of God's wisdom among humans. The early Christian hymn in Paul's Letter to the Colossians (1:15–20) uses images and phrases from those biblical poems to describe Jesus as the Wisdom of God: "the image of the invisible God, the firstborn of all creation" (1:15). Then it identifies the risen Jesus as the Wisdom of God ("the firstborn from the dead," 1:18), claims that the fullness of God dwells in him and affirms that by his death ("through the blood of his cross," 1:20) God has reconciled all creation to himself.

Another early Christian hymn, this one at the beginning of John's Gospel, celebrates Jesus as "the Word of God" (1:1–18). It describes him in terms of what the Old Testament poems say about the figure of Wisdom. It also introduces the master theme of John's Gospel: Jesus is both the revealer and the revelation of God. In other words, God has spoken definitively through the Word who has become flesh. And if we wish to know who God is and what God wants to tell us, we must listen to Jesus as the Word of God.

Titles

The New Testament writings apply many titles or honorific names to Jesus. Some, like "Prophet" and "Teacher," reflect the activities of Jesus during his earthly ministry. We have seen already how early hymns celebrated Jesus as the "Servant of God" and the "Wisdom of God." Still, other titles like "Son of God" and "Lord" express his extraordinary dignity during his earthly career and especially after his resurrection.

What are we today to make of all these different titles? No one of them exhausts the identity of Jesus. But each one of them expresses an aspect of the person of Jesus. Just as a diamond's many facets reveal its beauty when viewed from different angles, so the many titles of Jesus reveal different aspects of his person and allow us to see more clearly who he really was.

The titles "Christ" or "Messiah"—both mean "the Anointed One" in Greek and Hebrew, respectively—quickly became associated with Jesus. In Paul's letters "Christ" had practically become Jesus' second name. Rooted in Jesus' identity as a legal descendant of King David through Joseph, the title "Messiah" was very likely applied to Jesus by some of his fellow Jews who were impressed by his healing powers and were hoping that he would emerge as a powerful king for Israel. However, by his willing acceptance of suffering and death, Jesus redefined what it meant to be the Messiah of Israel.

The title "Son of Man" is used in three contexts in the Gospels: as Jesus' way of identifying himself, in connection with the predictions of his passion and death, and as a description of a glorious figure who will preside at the Last Judgment. "Son of Man" has deep roots in the Old Testament. It expresses Jesus' humanity as a "Son of Adam" (Ezekiel) and his role as a key figure in the full coming of God's kingdom (Daniel).

The title "Son of God" appears in the Old Testament in connection with the king at his coronation (Psalm 2) and with Israel as the people of God. Applying the title to Jesus was surely rooted in his own relationship of intimacy with God as his heavenly Father and in his invitation to his followers to address God with the title "Father."

The title "Lord" reflects early Christian beliefs about the divinity of Jesus. The Greek Old Testament uses "Lord" *(kyrios)* to translate the Hebrew Bible's term for God, "Yahweh." The oldest verse in the New Testament (1 Thessalonians 1:1) refers to "the Lord Jesus Christ." This way of talking about Jesus appears all through the New Testament letters, suggesting that the title "Lord" was commonly accepted among early Christians. Finally, John's Gospel begins with the affirmation that "the Word was God" (1:1) and reaches its climax with the apostle Thomas's confession that Jesus is "my Lord and my God" (20:28).

Sacraments

The two distinctive—even defining—rituals in early Christianity were baptism and the Eucharist. At the root of both sacraments was the belief that in and through them believers can participate in the life of the risen Jesus.

Jesus began his public life by accepting the baptism administered by John the Baptist. John seems to have served as an inspiration and a mentor for Jesus, and Jesus continued John's work of proclaiming the coming kingdom of God and challenging people to prepare for it.

Early Christian baptism surely had a basis in John's baptism. However, in light of Jesus' death and resurrection it quickly received a new theological meaning. It came to be understood as the ritual in which people of faith entered into the mystery of Jesus' death and resurrection (see Romans 6:3–4) and thus into the life of the Holy Trinity (see Matthew 28:19).

One of the most controversial features of Jesus' public ministry was his practice of sharing meals, often with socially and religiously "marginal" persons such as tax collectors and sinners. To some extent, these meals were "enacted parables" or symbolic demonstrations of the banquet to be celebrated in the fullness of God's kingdom.

At his Last Supper, the night before Jesus died, he identified the bread with his body and the wine with his blood. That meal became a preview of his passion and death, and the Eucharist celebrated in early Christian communities came to be understood as both the memorial of Jesus' Last Supper (and his death and resurrection) and the preview of the messianic banquet in God's kingdom. The Eucharist is the sacrament of ongoing Christian life by which we participate in the life of the risen Christ.

The first years after Jesus' death and resurrection constituted more of an explosion than a development in the Christian church. The professions of faith about Jesus and his significance for us, the hymns celebrating him as God's Servant and as the Wisdom of God, the many titles applied to Jesus in order to express the richness of his person and the rituals of baptism and the Eucharist—all of these arose within twenty years after his death on the cross. The extraordinary speed with which the language, theology and practices of the early Christians emerged is an eloquent witness to the power of Jesus' person and his resurrection.

. . . .

J U S T   A   M A N ?

Mary Magdalene received much of the publicity when *The Da Vinci Code* was released, but a far more significant controversy for Christians lies in another claim made by the novel's mysterious "scholar" Leigh Teabing. He reported that Jesus' early followers never considered him divine, that it wasn't until the time of Constantine that such claims were made—and then for political reasons involving Constantine's control of the church.

One of the most persistent heresies in the church from the earliest centuries through our own is the denial of one or the other of Jesus' two natures: human and divine. Docetism, for example, taught that Jesus only appeared to be human but was actually pure spirit and left the body before it was crucified. The heresy of Arianism claimed that Jesus was not co-eternal with the Father but had been created later. Arianism was resoundingly refuted by Athanasius. At the Council of Nicaea (AD 325), all but three bishops voted for Athanasius's position. This is why, in the Nicene Creed, we profess our belief in the Son who was "true God from true God, begotten not made...".

Some contemporary secular scholars still advance the position that Jesus was just a good and charismatic teacher of the first century. In their steadfast quest for the Jesus of history, they lose the significance of the Christ proclaimed by faith.

. . . .

QUESTIONS

• Which title for Jesus means the most to you in your faith life right now? What does this reveal about your relationship with God?

• Why do you think baptism and Eucharist were the first sacraments to be ritualized in the early Christian community? How can the special significance of these sacraments rouse your own baptismal call and participation in the Eucharist?

• The early church didn't slowly develop—it "exploded." The first Christians must have been truly enlivened by their faith in Jesus Christ. In what area does your faith need new life? What can you do to bring this about?

CHAPTER TWELVE

· *The Second Coming of Jesus* ·

The traditional profession of faith we Catholics and other Christians recite every Sunday concludes the section devoted to Jesus with these words: "He will come again in glory to judge the living and the dead, and his kingdom will have no end."[14] This faith statement concerns the second coming of Christ and his role in the Last Judgment and in the eternal kingdom of God.

The first coming of Christ involved Jesus' birth, life and death in the land of Israel some two thousand years ago. Through the Gospels we can learn a good deal about the historical Jesus. The result is that we can know as much—if not more—about Jesus as we know about almost any other figure from antiquity.

The Second Coming of Christ, however, is different. It is still to come, and it will involve the end of this age or world as we know it. This topic is the domain of prophets, not of historians who generally

JESUS : A HISTORICAL PORTRAIT

deal with the past and assume that it was much like the present. Nevertheless, historical study can at least tell us what people in the past imagined the future would be like, and in particular what early Christians believed about the Second Coming of Jesus and his place in the end times.

Eschatology and Apocalypse

Eschatology is the study of the "last things." In the context of ancient Judaism and Christianity, eschatology concerned the end of human history, the resurrection of the dead, the Last Judgment and subsequent rewards and punishments. The early Christians believed the risen Jesus would play a pivotal role when these events take place. This led to belief in the Second Coming of Christ.

Eschatology is often the content of many apocalypses. An *apocalypse* (derived from the Greek word for "revelation") is a narrative or story that describes a revelation about the future or the heavenly realm. It can take the form of a dream or a vision. There is often an angel who helps the visionary to interpret the experience. Many apocalypses claim to describe the future course of history and the unfolding of eschatological events.

Two books in the Bible are generally regarded as apocalypses: Daniel and Revelation. The Old Testament book of Daniel consists of reports about dreams and visions that gave hope and encouragement to Jews in the second century BC. They were undergoing severe persecution at the hands of the Syrian king Antiochus IV Epiphanes. The message of Daniel was this: Hold on, stay faithful and wait for God's help. Soon the kingdom of God will be made manifest to all creation, and the wise and righteous will shine "like the stars forever and ever" (12:1–3).

The book of Revelation also arose in a time of persecution. In the late first century AD Christians in western Asia Minor (present-day Turkey) were being forced to participate in rituals honoring the Roman emperor as a god. The visions granted to John and recorded in Revelation take as their starting point John's experience of the risen Jesus. They describe in various ways how the enemies of God's people will be overcome and how in the New Jerusalem the Lamb of God, the risen Jesus, will reign in glory with his heavenly Father. Both Daniel and Revelation emerged from situations of oppression and suffering. Both provided images of hope about the future and reasons for remaining faithful in the present.

The Glorious Son of Man

In Daniel 7 we see an imaginative and influential portrayal of divine judgment, where the prophet is allowed a glimpse of the heavenly court complete with a number of thrones. God, described as the "Ancient One," takes his place on the most glorious throne of all. All the heavenly beings are gathered "in judgment, / and the books were opened" (7:10). These books presumably contain the records of the deeds of those who are to be judged.

In this case the one to be judged is the wicked persecutor of Israel in the second century BC, King Antiochus IV, along with other enemies of God's people. In the midst of the court session, Daniel sees one "like a human being" (probably the archangel Michael) approaching the Ancient One. In response, the Ancient One gives the angel "dominion / and glory and kingship" (7:14).

A more literal translation of "like a human being" is "a son of man," meant to describe any human person and, in a sense, applicable to every one of us. However, the context of Daniel 7 in which "son of man" occurs endows it with the sense of a glorious being at home in the heavenly court and the recipient of "dominion and glory and kingship" from God.

When early Christians thought of the risen Jesus as the Son of Man, they envisioned him not so much as an ordinary human being as they did as the one raised from the dead, exalted to the heavens and worshiped as "our Lord Jesus Christ." And they associated him with the Last Judgment (for which resurrection was a precondition).

This idea of a worldwide Last Judgment—one that will mark the end of human history as we know it and involve rewards for the righteous and punishments for the wicked—developed from the Old Testament theme of the "day of the LORD." Prophets such as Amos sought to console the oppressed people by focusing on a time when the God of Israel will punish the wicked within his people and/or the enemies of Israel (5:18–20).

The Second Coming of Christ

The Second Coming of Christ is sometimes called the "Parousia." The Greek word *parousia* means "presence," "arrival," "advent" or "coming." It originally described the arrival of a king or high government official at a village or town for some kind of inspection. But *parousia* took on new meaning for early Christians. They used the word to describe the role they envisioned for the risen Jesus at the last judgment and the events surrounding it.

Again, a look at the earliest document in the New Testament—Paul's First Letter to the Thessalonians—written in AD 51, shows that belief in the Second Coming of Jesus was part of Christian faith from earliest days. Paul regarded the Thessalonians as a special source of hope for himself "before our Lord Jesus at his coming" (1 Thessalonians 2:19).

In his scenario for the end of this age and the Last Judgment, Paul assigned a prominent role to the risen Jesus and envisioned eternal life as being with him forever (4:13–18). He also warned that "the day of the Lord will come like a thief in the night" (5:2), that is, suddenly and when it is least expected. For Paul and the early Christians, the Second Coming was certain. But since no one knows the exact time, we should be prepared for it always.

Early Christians looked forward to the Second Coming of Christ as a stage in the fulfillment of their hopes for eternal life in the kingdom of God. They even devised a short prayer in Aramaic, *Maranatha*, which means "Our Lord, come!" This prayer appears in

Aramaic at the end of 1 Corinthians (16:22) and in Greek in Revelation 22:20. The use of Aramaic, the language of Jesus, suggests that the prayer originated very early in the history of the Christian movement. Its occurrence at the end of two New Testament books, among other prayers and greetings, suggests that it was well-known and widely accepted.

The Gospels of Matthew, Mark and Luke contain apocalyptic sermons in which Jesus outlines the events leading up to his Second Coming and the fullness of God's kingdom. These discourses contain many features and themes found in Daniel and Revelation, as well as in other Jewish apocalypses not contained in the Bible.

These apocalyptic accounts in the Gospels insist that while these future events *will* take place, no one except the Father knows their precise time. As with Paul, the Gospels' constant message is: Always be prepared. Live as if the Last Judgment were to occur in the next moment. Then you will have no need to fear that judgment.

The Last Judgment

The Gospel accounts about the Last Judgment give a prominent position to the glorious Son of Man. The imagery comes from Daniel 7:14, where the one "like a son of man" is given "dominion and glory and kingship." However, it is clear that the Gospel writers identified the glorious Son of Man as the risen Jesus and viewed his pivotal role in these future events as part of his second coming.

The climax of the apocalyptic discourse in Matthew is the judgment scene in 25:31–46. In it, the glorious Son of Man—the risen Jesus—serves as the judge of "all the nations." His task is to separate the righteous (the sheep) from the wicked (the goats).

The criteria that the glorious Son of Man will use in judging are deeds of kindness to "the least." Those deeds include the traditional works of mercy: feeding the hungry, giving drink to the thirsty, welcoming the stranger, clothing the naked, caring for the sick and visiting the imprisoned. Those who have done these deeds to "the least" will get to enjoy eternal life with God and the Son of Man, while those who neglected them will face eternal punishment. And in these scenes of meting out rewards and punishments, the one who passes judgment is the glorious Son of Man, the risen Christ.

Will these future events happen in exactly this way? The truth is, we don't know. It is very much the prerogative of God to bring about the fullness of the kingdom when and how God sees fit. However, Christians can be sure that whatever the exact sequence of events may be, the glorious risen Christ as "the firstborn from the dead" (Colossians 1:18; Revelation 1:5) will have a prominent position in them. This conviction, of course, flows from faith and hope, not from history.

Jesus taught us all to pray for the coming of the fullness of God's kingdom with the Lord's Prayer. In this prayer he gives us a vision of the future when all creation will celebrate the holiness of God and do God's will perfectly. He urges us to ask for divine help and guidance in the midst of the events that will lead to the fullness of God's kingdom.

He teaches us to pray, "Thy kingdom come." He advises us to look forward to that blessed day not as something to be feared but rather as something to be welcomed: "Now when these things begin to take place, stand up and raise your heads, because your redemption is drawing near" (Luke 21:28). Our Christian response can and should be the early Christian prayer: *Maranatha*—"Our Lord, come!"

· · · · · · · · · · · · · · · ·
ANTICIPATING THE
END TIMES

In 1996 Tim LaHaye and Jerry Jenkins published the first *Left Behind* novel. The series of a dozen novels has been described as "the absolute champion in the race to make the Book of Revelation into racy thriller reading."[15] But for all its popularity, the series remains fiction only loosely connected to the Bible. It has much deeper roots in fundamentalist Christianity's political agenda.

The concept of "the Rapture," first articulated in the nineteenth century, has no solid grounding in Scripture. Based loosely on metaphors in Paul's letters and a misunderstanding of the book of Revelation, it describes an evil world left to be punished by God after the saved have been taken up into the clouds.

The Gospels and Paul's writings tell us again and again that no one knows the day or the hour of Christ's Second Coming. As Catholic Christians, we do not believe in literalistic interpretation of the Bible. Still less do we spin such an interpretation into a fictional description of the end times, relishing the punishment of those who don't share our views. Rather, we follow Jesus Christ who says that the kingdom of God is even now in our midst. Our love for one another and justice toward all are signs of that kingdom, which will reach its fulfillment when Jesus comes in glory.

· · · · · · · · · · · · · · · · · ·

QUESTIONS

- How do you envision the Second Coming of Christ and the Last Judgment? Do you fear it or welcome it? How does your relationship with God affect your vision of the end of the world?

- Should we read the visions of the end times in Daniel and the book of Revelation as literal descriptions of what is to come or as purely symbolic messages of hope?

- How are you preparing for the Second Coming? What more can you do for "the least" to ensure your place among the sheep and enjoyment of eternal life?

CONCLUSION

"The Word became flesh and lived among us." Those words from John 1:14 provide the biblical warrant for the historical study about Jesus described in this little book and in all the big books listed in the bibliography beginning on page 115. According to Christian faith, the Word of God became human in a specific time (about 4 BC) and in a specific place (the land of Israel, or Palestine). As the Word of God, Jesus of Nazareth was the revealer of God (whom he addressed as "Father") and the revelation of God (in that he showed us who God is and what God wants of us).

While surrounded with difficulties, the historical study of Jesus provides a solid foundation for what the New Testament writers and Christians believe about Jesus. Believers have nothing to fear from serious historical study. Indeed, in the light of such historical research on Jesus and what it reveals about him, we can make our own the rest of John 1:14: "and we have seen his glory, the glory as of a father's only son, full of grace and truth."

APPENDIX

· *Jesus and the Dead Sea Scrolls* ·

The discovery of the Dead Sea Scrolls in Palestine in the late 1940s has been described as the greatest archaeological find in history. The most important texts are from the site known as Qumran. Besides giving us the earliest manuscripts of the Hebrew Bible, the Qumran library has provided original Hebrew and Aramaic texts of various Jewish writings outside the Bible, biblical commentaries, retellings of biblical texts and Aramaic translations of some Hebrew biblical texts. Most surprising of all were previously unknown Jewish religious community rules and related sectarian documents (hymns and wisdom instructions, for example).

The Qumran scrolls date from the second century BC to the first century AD. The site of Qumran was most likely a center for a Jewish religious group, and it is highly probable that there was a relationship between the group that inhabited the site and the scrolls discovered in the eleven caves surrounding it. The Qumran scrolls are the remnants of the library of the Jewish religious group that settled there. This group, if we can judge from the scrolls, was both priestly and apocalyptic in orientation. From the first discoveries the group was identified as the Essenes, already familiar from descriptions in the writings of Josephus and Philo.

Jesus was not an Essene, and certainly not one of the Qumran type. Galilee is some distance from the Dead Sea, and according to the Gospels Jesus spent nearly all his life and most of his public ministry in Galilee. If there was any Essene influence on him, it may have come through John the Baptist.

The principal significance of the Qumran scrolls for research on Jesus is that they provide parallels to Jesus and his movement. They can tell us what was "in the air" in the time of Jesus. By comparing them with what is known about Jesus, it is possible to receive some illumination about what were apparently two independent movements within first-century Palestinian Judaism. What follows gives particular attention to what are regarded as "sectarian" texts in the Qumran library: the Rule of the Community (1QS), Thanksgiving Hymns (1QH), War Scroll (1QM), Habakkuk Pesher, Messianic Rule (1QSa) and Damascus Document (CD).[16]

The Jesus Movement

John's characteristic ritual of baptism suggests a link to the Qumran community. Members of the community addressed in the Rule of the Community practiced a ritual of spiritual cleansing symbolized by the use of water (1QS 3:8–9). The regular practice of ritual cleansing of body and soul at Qumran is confirmed by archaeological excavations that uncovered an intricate system of water channels that made these "baptisms" possible.

If there is a historical link between Jesus and the Qumran community, the most likely candidate is John the Baptist. According to Luke 1:80, John lived and was active in the Judean desert. He practiced a "baptism" or ritual washing that signified repentance and the forgiveness of sins. Jesus submitted to John's baptism and very likely took John as his mentor. According to John 4:1, Jesus was "baptizing more disciples than John."

Nevertheless, the idea that John the Baptist was the conduit between the Qumran community and Jesus is only an intriguing possibility. The Judean desert at this time seems to be home to many Jewish religious movements, and so there is no certainty that John was ever part of the Qumran community or an Essene. And even if he was, John set out on his own path and founded a new movement.[17] Moreover, John's baptism seems to have been once-for-all-time moral preparation for the imminent coming of God's kingdom, whereas at Qumran "baptism" appears to have been repeated ritually. At any rate, Jesus in turn went his own way from John, and practiced a very different style of ministry in the service of the coming kingdom of God.

From the start the Jesus movement involved a community of disciples. However, the Gospels provide little data about the structures and institutions of the earliest Jesus movement. By contrast, the Qumran Rule of the Community (1QS) and the Damascus Document (CD) offer much information about the structures and institutions of the Jewish religious movement(s) that they purport to represent. The former text envisions a secluded and almost "monastic" setting, whereas the latter presupposes a community life lived out within the broader society of Jews and Gentiles.

According to the Rule of the Community, prospective members presented themselves to enter the group and had to pass through a two-year period of testing before their full acceptance. The "master" served as their spiritual leader, and the rule was apparently written for him to use as a handbook. The community had a strong priestly spirituality and practiced frequent ritual purifications and shared meals. The priestly character of the group was reinforced during its meetings and meals where a strict hierarchical order beginning with the priests was maintained. The rule deals with offenses ranging from blasphemy to sleeping during the community meetings. Within the group there was an inner circle consisting of twelve men (representing the twelve tribes of Israel) and three priests (representing the three priestly families that traced their ancestry back to Aaron).

The vocabulary and ideas of the Damascus Document link it to the Rule of the Community. But the second part of the work ("the statutes") presupposes a setting in which those who live in the "camps" of the community have contact with nonmembers. The statutes deal with oaths, lost property, purification, Sabbath observance and various other topics. The section about the organization of the community (CD 12:19–14:19) gives prominence to the "guardian" of the camp—the official who instructs the congregation, exercises pastoral care, examines candidates and oversees the affairs of the community. His Hebrew title *mebaqqer* ("overseer") is equivalent to *episkopos* in Greek, the early Christian word for "bishop."

Inclusive table fellowship seems to have been a characteristic and controversial feature of Jesus' public ministry. These meals served to model and anticipate life in God's kingdom, functioning as previews of the messianic banquet. A Qumran document known as the "Rule for the Last Days" or "Messianic Rule" (1QSa) provides a description of a community meal that features bread and wine, and involves the participation of two anointed figures or "messiahs." In this meal the priestly and hierarchical character of the group is clear. The "Priest"—previously identified as the "Priest-Messiah"—is the first to bless the bread and wine. Then the Messiah of Israel (a David figure) extends his hand over the bread, and the congregation utters a blessing. In the double messianism presupposed by this text the Priest-Messiah has precedence. The meal itself has a ritual character and serves as a preview or anticipation of the messianic banquet to be celebrated in the fullness of God's kingdom. The description of the meal is followed by a directive: "It is according to this statute that they shall proceed at every meal at which at least ten are gathered together" (1QSa 2:21–22). This suggests that every community meal carries messianic significance and eschatological overtones and somehow anticipates and points toward the fullness of God's kingdom.

So it appears that the meals of the messiahs of Aaron and David and of Jesus the Messiah take place as signs of the fullness of God's reign. The fundamental difference, of course, comes in the open table fellowship of Jesus. His meals are open especially to marginal persons such as tax collectors and sinners, whereas the meals described in 1QSa seem to be for members only. Moreover, at Jesus' meals he is the one presiding figure, who combines the roles of the priestly and Davidic messiahs.

While Luke presents the Jerusalem temple as the house of Jesus, there are important indications in the Gospels that the historical Jesus stood in tension with the temple (Mark 11:15–19; 13:2). Indeed, these tensions contributed greatly to his death (see Mark 14:58). The conventional explanation for the founding of the Qumran community also involves tension with the Jerusalem temple. According to this theory, a Jewish group devoted to the temple took exception to the Maccabean usurpation of the high priesthood and control of the temple and went out to the Judean desert to await the divine intervention that would restore the authentic priesthood and purify the temple.

Even apart from this historical hypothesis, the Qumran texts themselves suggest that tension with the Jerusalem temple led the community to view itself as "the House of Holiness for Israel, an Assembly of Supreme Holiness for Aaron" (1QS 8:5–6) and to substitute prayer and good works for the traditional temple sacrifices. The work known as 4QMMT contains a list of legal disagreements between the Qumran people and those in charge of the Jerusalem temple about the temple and its rituals. The Temple Scroll provides a verbal blueprint for a new, ideal temple and temple city when the right people (God and the Sons of Light) will be in charge of it again. The New Jerusalem texts specify the dimensions of various features of the city. And 1 Enoch 91 and 93—a work well represented in the Qumran library—displays disappointment with the second temple.

The Teachings of Jesus

There is general agreement that the kingdom of God was central in Jesus' teaching and activity, that this kingdom was in the future (eschatological) and transcendent (God's kingdom), and that his teaching about the kingdom should be understood against the background of the Jewish apocalypses. When Mark came to summarize the preaching of Jesus, he placed the kingdom of God at the forefront (Mark 1:15).

The Qumran community shared the hopes of other Jews and of Jesus for the full manifestation of God's kingdom. The presence of multiple manuscripts of Daniel and 1 Enoch in the Qumran library shows a lively interest in apocalyptic thinking. While none of the "sectarian" works is a full-scale apocalypse, most of these texts contain abundant apocalyptic language and content.

The instruction in the Rule of the Community (1QS 3:13—4:26 explains how humans should act by way of preparation for the coming of God's kingdom. It establishes at the start the absolute sovereignty of God, claims that the world in the present age is under the control of two great figures (the Prince of Light and the Angel of Darkness), and promises that at God's visitation there will be vindication for the children of light and destruction for the children of darkness. How the visitation might happen is described in great imaginative detail in the Qumran War Scroll.

While the influence of this theological schema is most obvious in the Pauline and Johannine writings, there are at least hints that some elements of it were presuppositions for Jesus' proclamation of the kingdom of God. Jesus acknowledged the absolute sovereignty of the God of Israel, whom he called "Father." He viewed the present as a time of struggle on the individual and cosmic level in which the authority of God was at stake. And he looked forward to the decisive intervention of God when his prayer "Your kingdom come" would be answered.

The present dimension of God's kingdom resides in the ministry of Jesus himself. Jesus' claim "I saw Satan fall like lightning from heaven" (Luke 10:18) indicates that the final struggle was already underway and the victory was near. The belief that God raised Jesus from the dead assigns what was regarded as a collective and eschatological event to an individual before the other end-time events come to pass. And Jesus' wisdom instructions about entering the kingdom concern the kind of behavior that is appropriate against the horizon of the future fullness of God's kingdom.

There are elements of present eschatology in the Qumran scrolls. The most striking motif is the permeable boundary between heaven and earth. Through prayer or revelatory experiences it is possible for certain humans to enter the heavenly council. The Qumran wisdom texts place much of their advice in the framework of "the mystery that is to come"—a concept analogous to the New Testament's "kingdom of God." The Qumran wisdom texts make it clear that for the Qumran people (and other Jews) eschatology and ethics went together.

If not unparalleled, Jesus' teaching about loving one's enemies (Matthew 6:44; Luke 6:27) is unusual and characteristic of his core teachings. In Matthew 5:43 Jesus' teaching about love of enemies is introduced by a partial quotation of Leviticus 19:18 ("You shall love your neighbor") along with a curious addition ("and hate your enemy"), a clause found neither in Leviticus 19:18 nor elsewhere in the Old Testament. The Qumran Rule of the Community (1QS 1:10) proposes that members "may hate all the sons of darkness, each according to his guilt in God's vengeance." In the framework of the Rule of the Community the Sons of Darkness are polar opposites of the Sons of Light and are led by the Angel of Darkness to perform the deeds of darkness. As such they deserve the hatred of God and so the hatred of the Sons of Light (though 1QS 10:17–21 counsels a more tolerant attitude toward enemies).

By the criteria of dissimilarity and multiple attestations, the prohibition of divorce belongs to the corpus of Jesus' authentic sayings. The rabbis Hillel, Shammai and Aqiba all assumed the validity of divorce and argued about the grounds for divorce.[18] Two Qumran texts are often cited as background for or parallels to Jesus' radical teaching about no divorce. The Damascus Document 4:20—5:6 declares that "taking a second wife while the first is alive" is fornication. As in Mark 10:2–12 the biblical justification is the order of creation enunciated in Genesis 1:27: "[M]ale and female he created them." However, the topic at issue here seems to be polygamy rather than divorce and remarriage, since the rest of the passage is concerned to explain why David had several wives.

The Temple Scroll contains a long section about the king. With regard to marriage (11QT 57:15–19), the ideal king should marry within the royal household of Israel. The text goes on to say: "He shall not take another wife in addition to her, for she alone shall be with him all the time of her life." Again the "no divorce" interpretation is problematic. The first problem is whether the directive applies to anyone beyond the king. The second problem is whether it refers to polygamy on the king's part or to divorce and remarriage, though here the evidence for "no divorce" is stronger.

The Person of Jesus

With regard to Jesus' practice of addressing God as "Abba" (Father), two Qumran texts—neither of which seems to be "sectarian"—have both illuminated and complicated the matter. The psalm in 4Q372 1 begins with the address "My Father and my God." The speaker, who seems to be the patriarch Joseph, expresses confidence that God will be kindly disposed toward him and will save him from the hands of the gentiles. In this text we have solid evidence that in the literature of Palestinian Judaism "my Father" was used as a personal address to God by someone other than Jesus. Moreover, the context is similar to Jesus' own "Abba" prayer in Gethsemane (Mark 14:36), which continues with an expression of confidence in God ("for you all things are possible") and issues in a petition.

That the title "Son of God" was not the creation of Greek mythology but rather belongs within Palestinian Judaism has been confirmed by the Qumran Aramaic "Son of God" text (4Q246). In this text someone is described as follows: "The Son of God he will be proclaimed [or: proclaim himself], and the Son of the Most High they will call him." The language sounds very much like the angel Gabriel's annunciation to Mary in Luke 1:32–35. The problem with 4Q246 comes in identifying the one about whom these statements are being made. It is, of course, hard to resist a "messianic" interpretation or least a reference to the "one like a Son of Man" in Daniel 7 (which is the context of 4Q246). However, it is also possible (given the fragmentary condition of the manuscript) that it deals with a historical figure. This possibility in turn raises the question whether the historical figure might be a friend of Israel or an enemy. The ambiguity, however, need not obscure what is most important: the presence of the titles "Son of God" and "Son of the Most High" in a Palestinian Jewish text prior to the composition of the New Testament.

Two texts from the Qumran library supply information about crucifixion. The Pesher on Nahum (4Q169) refers to "the furious young lion" (the Seleucid king Demetrius III Eukairos, who ruled from 95 to 75 BC) as the one who "hangs men alive" and to "a man hanged alive on a tree" (frgs. 3–4 i 6–7). The "hanging" most likely refers to crucifixion. The Temple Scroll (11QT 64:6–13) prescribes crucifixion as the appropriate punishment for those who betray the Jewish people ("they shall hang him on the tree") and for apostates who had committed capital crimes ("you shall hang him on the tree"). Here we must assume that Jewish officials had some part in these crucifixions. The latter text has led both Jewish and Christian scholars to reopen the discussion about possible Jewish involvement in Jesus' death, though the ultimate legal responsibility of Pontius Pilate for Jesus' crucifixion seems well-established.

In many of the "sectarian" texts among the Qumran manuscripts a figure known as "the Teacher of Righteousness" or "the Righteous Teacher" is prominent. According to the Damascus Document, God "raised up for them a Teacher of Righteousness to guide them in the way of His heart" (1:11). According to the Commentary on Habakkuk, God made known to the Teacher of Righteousness "all the mysteries of the words of His servants the Prophets" (1QpHab 7:4–5) and will rescue the community "because of their suffering and because of their faith in the Teacher of Righteousness" (1QpHab 8:2–3).

The Thanksgiving Hymns may be the most important source for information about the Teacher of Righteousness, if we follow the line of interpretation that their abundant first-person singular language refers to the Teacher. Thus they would provide in part the "memoirs" of the Teacher ("I") with their references to his experiences of divine revelation, his opposition from "lying interpreters" and "those who seek smooth things" (probably the Pharisees), his participation in the heavenly council, and his pastoral solicitude for other members of the group.

Jesus and the Teacher of Righteousness were central figures in two Jewish religious movements that flourished in late Second Temple times. Both were regarded (and surely regarded themselves) as recipients of divine revelation about the "mysteries" of God and his kingdom. Both suffered from opponents within the Jewish people. Both provided the wise teachings and spiritual energy that insured that their memories would be preserved and that their movements would continue.

On the basis of these parallels some have argued that Jesus was really the Teacher of Righteousness or that the Teacher provided the precedent and pattern for Jesus. There are, however, some important differences. The Teacher of Righteousness was a Jewish priest active in Judea around 150 BC who shaped a Jewish sect that in turn preserved his memory. Jesus of Nazareth was a Jewish layman active principally in Galilee around AD 30 who shaped a religious movement that eventually became open to Jews and to gentiles who in turn preserved his memory. Jesus' movement proclaimed that Jesus was raised from the dead and reigns as the "Lord Jesus Christ." That is a very important difference.

BIBLIOGRAPHY

Allison, Dale C. *The Sermon on the Mount: Inspiring the Moral Imagination.* New York: Crossroad, 1999.

Bauckham, Richard and Trevor Hart. *Hope Against Hope: Christian Eschatology at the Turn of the Millennium.* Grand Rapids: Eerdmans, 1999.

Bovon, François. *The Last Days of Jesus.* Louisville: Westminster John Knox, 2006.

Brown, Raymond E. *The Birth of the Messiah.* New York: Doubleday, 1993.

———. *The Death of the Messiah,* vols. 1 and 2. New York: Doubleday, 1994 and 1999.

———. *An Introduction to New Testament Christology.* New York: Paulist, 1994.

Bryan, Christopher. *Render to Caesar: Jesus, the Early Church, and the Roman Superpower.* New York: Oxford University Press, 2005.

Chilton, Bruce D., ed. *The Kingdom of God in the Teaching of Jesus.* Philadelphia: Fortress, 1984.

Collins, John J. *The Apocalyptic Imagination: An Introduction to Jewish Apocalyptic Literature.* Grand Rapids: Eerdmans, 1998.

Cotter, Wendy. *Miracles in Greco-Roman Antiquity: A Sourcebook for the Study of New Testament Miracle Stories.* London: Routledge, 1999.

Cullmann, Oscar. *Prayer in the New Testament.* Minneapolis: Fortress, 1995.

Donahue, John R. *The Gospel in Parable: Metaphor, Narrative, and Theology in the Synoptic Gospels.* Minneapolis: Fortress, 1990.

Dunn, James D. G. *Jesus Remembered.* Grand Rapids: Eerdmans, 2003.

Freyne, Sean. *Jesus, a Jewish Galilean: A New Reading of the Jesus Story.* London: T&T Clark, 2005.

Hengel, Martin. *Crucifixion in the Ancient World and the Folly of the Message of the Cross.* Philadelphia: Augsburg Fortress, 1977.

Hoppe, Leslie. *There Shall Be No Poor Among You: Poverty in the Bible.* Nashville: Abingdon, 2004.

Horsley, Richard A. *Jesus and the Spiral of Violence: Popular Jewish Resistance in Roman Palestine.* Minneapolis: Augsburg Fortress, 1992.

Houlden, Leslie L., ed. *Jesus. The Complete Guide.* New York: Continuum, 2006.

Hurtado, Larry W. *Lord Jesus Christ: Devotion to Jesus in Earliest Christianity.* Grand Rapids: Eerdmans, 2006.

Johnson, Elizabeth A. *Truly Our Sister: A Theology of Mary in the Communion of Saints.* New York: Continuum, 2003.

Johnson, Luke T. *Religious Experience in Earliest Christianity: A Missing Dimension in New Testament Studies.* Minneapolis: Augsburg Fortress, 1998.

Karris, Robert J. *Prayer and the New Testament: Jesus and His Communities at Worship.* New York: Crossroad, 2000.

Kiley, Mark et al., eds. *Prayer from Alexander to Constantine: A Critical Anthology.* London: Routledge, 1997.

McKnight, Scot. *Jesus and His Death: Historiography, the Historical Jesus, and Atonement Theory.* Waco, Tex.: Baylor University Press, 2005.

Meier, John P. *A Marginal Jew: Rethinking the Historical Jesus.* vols. 1–3. New York: Doubleday, 1991–2001.

Perkins, Pheme. *Resurrection: New Testament Witness and Contemporary Reflection.* New York: Doubleday, 1984.

Sanders, E.P. *Jesus and Judaism.* Minneapolis: Augsburg Fortress, 1985.

Schüssler Fiorenza, Elisabeth. *In Memory of Her: A Feminist Theological Reconstruction of Christian Origins.* New York: Continuum, 1994.

Schweitzer, Albert. *The Quest of the Historical Jesus.* W. Montgomery, trans. Mineola, N.Y.: Dover, 2005.

Segal, Alan. *Life After Death: A History of the Afterlife in Western Religions.* New York: Doubleday, 2004.

Theissen, Gerd. *The Religion of the Earliest Churches: Creating a Symbolic World.* John Bowden, trans. Minneapolis: Augsburg Fortress, 1999.

Twelftree, Graham H. *Jesus the Miracle Worker: A Historical and Theological Study.* Downers Grove, Ill.: InterVarsity, 1999.

Vermes, Geza. *The Complete Dead Sea Scrolls in English.* New York: Penguin, 2006.

Viviano, Benedict. *The Kingdom of God in History.* Eugene, Oreg.: Wipf and Stock, 2002.

Weaver, Walter P. *The Historical Jesus in the Twentieth Century, 1900-1950.* Harrisburg, Pa.: Trinity Press International, 1999.

Witherington, Ben. *Jesus the Sage: The Pilgrimage of Wisdom.* Minneapolis: Augsburg Fortress, 1994.

Wright, N.T. *Jesus and the Victory of God.* Minneapolis: Augsburg Fortress, 1997.

————. *The Resurrection of the Son of God.* Minneapolis: Augsburg Fortress, 2003.

NOTES

1. Flavius Josephus, *Jewish Antiquities,* Loeb Classical Library, trans. (Cambridge, Mass.: Harvard University Press, 1963), 18:63–64.

2. See John P. Meier, *A Marginal Jew: Rethinking the Historical Jesus* (New York: Doubleday, 1991).

3. See N.T. Wright, *Jesus and the Victory of God* (Minneapolis: Augsburg Fortress, 1997).

4. Flavius Josephus, *Jewish Antiquities,* 18:116–117.

5. Hans Küng, *The Church* (New York: Sheed and Ward, 1968), p. 90.

6. The Sacramentary, *The Roman Missal,* The Order of Mass, Communion Rite, Lord's Prayer, International Commission on English in the Liturgy, trans. (New York: Catholic Book Publishing, 1985), p. 561.

7. Daniel J. Harrington, *The Gospel of Matthew* (Collegeville, Minn.: Liturgical, 1991) p. 276.

8. Raymond E. Brown, *The Death of the Messiah* (New York: Doubleday, 1991).

9. Philo, *Embassy to Gaius,* 301.

10. Austin Flannery, o.p., *Vatican II: The Conciliar and Post Conciliar Documents,* Declaration on the Relation of the Church to Non-Christian Religions *(Nostra Aetate)* no. 4, (Northport, N.Y.: Costello, 1996), p. 741.

11. National Conference of Catholic Bishops' Committee for Ecumenical and Interreligious Affairs, "Criteria for the Evaluation of Dramatizations of the Passion," no. A1, (Washington, D.C.: United States Catholic Conference, 1988), p. 3.

12. The Sacramentary, The Order of the Mass, Eucharistic Prayer Prefaces, Christian Death I, p. 527.

13. Pliny, *Letters,* 10.96.

14. The Sacramentary, The Order of the Mass, The Liturgy of the Word, Profession of Faith, p. 368.

15. Amazon.com editorial review for Tim F. LaHaye and Jerry B. Jenkins, *Left Behind: A Novel of the Earth's Last Days* (Carol Stream, Ill.: Tyndale House, 1995). Review available at http://www.amazon.com.

16. Excerpts from the Dead Sea Scrolls have been taken from Geza Vermes, *The Complete Dead Sea Scrolls in English* (New York: Penguin, 1997).

17. See Flavius Josephus, *Jewish Antiquities,* 18:116–119.

18. Jacob Neusner, *The Mishnah: A New Translation* (New Haven, Conn.: Yale University Press, 1988), 9:10, p. 487.

prayer
  Apostles' Creed, 69
  Eighteen Benedictions, 46, 47
  Jesus' practice of, 45, 47–52
  in Jewish worship, 46
  Kaddish, 46, 47
  Lord's Prayer. *See* Lord's Prayer.
  in Luke, 45, 46, 47, 49
  Maranatha, 96, 98
  at Mass, 51–52
  in Matthew, 47–48
  Nicene Creed, 91
  psalms, 45
  Shema, 46
  Shemoneh Esreh, 46. *See also*
    Eighteen Benedictions *under
    this heading.*
precious pearl, parable of. *See under*
  parables.
Promised Land. *See* Holy Land.
Protestantism
  German, 10
Proverbs, book of, 33
psalms. *See under* prayer.

Q source, 11
Quelle, 11
Qumran, 32

"Rapture," 99
Ratzinger, Joseph (Pope Benedict
  XVI), 44
Revelation, book of, 65, 94, 95,
  97, 99
Romans, Letter to the, 86
Roman Empire, 20, 22, 27, 62–63,
  64–65, 71, 74

Sadducees, 16, 79
Samaria, 13
Saul, 22, 28
scribes, 16
Sea of Galilee, 9, 18, 41, 42
Seleucid Greeks, 62, 111
Sepphoris, 15
Sermon on the Mount, 32–33, 38
Shammai, 110
Sheol, 78
Simeon, 54
Simon Peter, 18. *See also* Peter.
Sirach, book of, 33
Solomon, 62
Stephen, 70
stoning, 70. *See also* Stephen.
Susanna, 55
Syrophoenician woman, 41, 56

tax collectors, 16
"Teaching of the Twelve Apostles,"
  52
tekton, defined, 15
Therapeutae, 57
Thessalonians, Letters to the, 96
Thomas
  appearance of Jesus to, 81
  Infancy Gospel of Thomas, 12
Thomas, Gospel of, 7, 11

wheat and weeds, parable of. *See
  under* parables.
Wright, N.T., 17

yeast, parable of. *See under* parables.

Zealots, 16, 27, 63, 67
Zechariah, 17
Zechariah, book of, 35

SCRIPTURE INDEX

	20:20–26	63
	21:28	98
	23:46	47
John	1:1	89
	1:1–18	88
	1:14	101
	1:35–42	18
	1:36	18
	1:46	15
	3:2	21
	17	51
	17:1	51
	19:6	74
	20:28	89
Acts	2:13	77
	7:54–60	70
	17:32	77
Romans	3:25	87
	6:3–4	89
	13:1–7	4
	13:3–4	86
1 Corinthians	6:4–8	83
	7:8	58
	7:38	58
	15:3–5	86
	15:3–8	81
	15:4	82
	15:20, 22	83
	16:22	97
Galatians	3:28	87
Philippians	2:6–11	87
	2:11	87
Colossians	1:15	88
	1:15–20	87
	1:18	88, 98
	1:20	88
1 Thessalonians	1:1	89
	2:19	96
	4:13–18	96
	5:2	96
Revelation	1:5	98
	22:20	97